COPING WITH

Being Adopted

Shari Cohen

THE ROSEN PUBLISHING GROUP, INC. NEW YORK

Published in 1988 by The Rosen Publishing Group, Inc.
29 East 21st Street, New York, NY 10010

Copyright 1988 by Shari Cohen

First Edition

Library of Congress Cataloging-in-Publication Data

Cohen, Shari.
    Coping with being adopted.

    Bibliography: p.
    Includes index.
    Summary: Discusses feelings and questions associated with being adopted, taking into account both birth parents and adoptive parents and dealing with the beginning, the end, and everything in between.
    1. Children, Adopted—Life skills guides—Juvenile literature.
2. Adoption—Psychological aspects—Juvenile literature. [1. Adoption]
I. Title.
HV875.C59 1987   362.7'33   87-23385
ISBN 0-8239-0770-8

Manufactured in the United States of America

*The love of a
family is
so uplifting*

*The warmth
of a family
is so comforting*

*The support
of a family
is so reassuring*

*The attitude
of a family
toward
each other
molds one's
attitudes
forever
toward the world.*

Susan Polis Schultz

ABOUT THE AUTHOR ◇

Shari Cohen is a free-lance writer whose human interest stories about people and events in her community have appeared in national newspapers and magazines. Recently she has been involved in writing television scripts specifically for the young adult audience. She is the author of two young adult specials, "The Fall of Jennifer Cool" and "Every Trick in the Book." Currently she is engaged in writing a series of novels for handicapped young adults.

A native of Minneapolis, she attended the University of Minnesota, where she majored in English and Journalism. In 1972 she moved to Los Angeles and began working for the federal government on the space program. She now lives in Woodland Hills, California, with her husband, Paul, and their three children, Barry, Adam, and Stephanie.

Contents

Introduction

Adolescence is a tough time for everyone. It is a time when you are coming to terms with certain questions about life and existence. It is a time when you are experiencing a wide range of emotions—hate, love, acceptance and rejection—and at the same time going through physical changes of voice, size, and shape. For those who have been adopted, asking the question "Who am I?" has added impact.

Who am I? What does my birth mother look like? Why did she give me away? These are some of the most frequently asked questions by children and young adults who have been adopted into families. Although the questions are universal and shared by many, some secret thoughts and feelings are kept quiet and shared with few. The desire to run away, for example. Or the feeling that you are the one in the family who has "bad blood" and that you carry with you a dark secret past.

In this book we shall talk about those feelings. We shall also talk about coping. About coping with upsetting remarks made by well-meaning friends and relatives. About the longing to know your true identity and the frustration of not being able to find out. When...where... how do you search for your origins? Should the attempt be made at all? And what about reunion, the coming together of birth parent and child? Who benefits most and why?

What are some of the feelings of adoptive parents? Many of them experience conflict within the family because of adoption-related problems.

Gathered together in this book is much information on these topics, as well as personal interviews with young people who have been adopted. While statistics and state laws speak for themselves, the most meaningful exploration was talking with the kids directly, hearing of their experiences, their fears, and their fantasies.

People living in the city and those living in rural areas are worlds apart in some of their ideas but linked together by a common bond. That bond is belonging, being loved and accepted in a family unit that was created especially for them, a unit that others often taken for granted.

Perhaps while reading this book you will see yourself in some of the situations described. You will see that feelings of rejection, failure, and abandonment are felt by others and can be overcome.

Many books that have been written about adoption deal with beginnings and endings. This one looks at everything in between. Are you ready? Let's explore. Together we will cover subjects of real parents, real problems, and perhaps discover along the way the *real you*.

CHAPTER 1

How It Feels

Movies have been made, articles written, and surveys compiled on the subject of how it feels to be adopted. Many people take the attitude that the adoptee is "lucky to be living with the new family," for where would the child be if it weren't for them? On the streets? In an institution?

Actors can portray the scene and neighbors can gossip, but the only true way of knowing how it feels to be adopted into a family is to hear it directly from the child or young adult: to hear of his/her hopes and expectations, to listen to his feelings and hear her speak of fantasies about the past and wishes for the future.

The following are personal insights into how it feels to be adopted. These young people are all still living at home. Many are happy and content in their home life as it is. Others are having problems with their parents, themselves, and the outside world in general. They are angry and resentful and have feelings of rejection and failure.

Some of them had questions themselves, such as learning their true identity and the whereabouts of their birth parents. When asked how it felt to be adopted, there were no hesitations, no requests for time to think the question over. The answers were direct and honest, spoken without malice or reservation.

I had always suspected that I was adopted because I didn't resemble anyone in my family. When I turned sixteen, I was told the truth. Although it didn't come as a complete surprise, I was really shaken up. It took me a long time to get over the fact that the couple who were raising me were not my "real" mom and dad.

Andrea, 18

The people who adopted me are the only parents I have ever known. They have been great and have given me everything. I sometimes wonder what it would have been like had I been raised by my "real" mother. I wonder what she looks like and if she ever thinks of me.

Lisa, 14

Every man in his thirties with red curly hair is my father. I imagine that I see him everywhere.

Sean, 15

My big plan is to wait until I'm eighteen, then split. I've been in trouble for as long as I can remember. Some of it was my fault, some of it wasn't. There will be no regrets when I leave. It will be a time for celebration. Everyone will be happy.

Brian, 16

I remember when I was in third grade. I had a fight with this girl and she yelled across the playground,

"You're mean, you're stupid, and you're adopted!" For a long time I felt that being adopted was something bad, something that set me apart from the others.

Anna, 15

My cousin once told me that my blood was different than the rest of the family's, that no one wanted to hurt my feelings by telling me that I really didn't belong. When I was younger I felt like an outcast at family parties. Even now, this cousin is cool and keeps his distance. He makes me feel like a freak.

Peter, 17

I'm always told that I am special. My parents are my parents. I love them. I would never leave them for my "real" parents.

Jill, 13

Being adopted is the greatest thing that could happen to someone. It means that someone hoped for you and waited a long time to get you.

Mia, 15

I'm just like everybody else except I don't know what my family history is. It's kinda scary that something could happen to me, like maybe I'd need some blood or something and no one would know where to get it or whatever. I mean, that's scary. . .or I could end up falling in love with my brother!

Sara, 14

Being adopted is sometimes like you've got a strange disease and other times completely normal, but there's usually no one to talk to about it, really, because everyone treats you like you're weird.

Tim, 13

Why do people have babies if they don't want them? I'm lucky somebody took me in. . .I could have stayed in an orphanage or foster home or something awful like that. I'm very lucky.

Ginny, 14

I was given up for adoption because my mom was too young to raise a child. I don't *ever* want to have kids, but if I do, I won't ever give them away no matter what!

Lilian, 16

I don't want to make my parents feel bad—as if I liked my real parents more than them. They do a lot to help me, so I'm better off keeping things the way they are.

Joan, 17

It is said that the primary purpose of adoption is to create a new parent-child relationship that will provide a wholesome opportunity for the child's growth and development. It sounds easy enough, but it's not that simple. If it were, there would be no discontent, no rebellion or conflict within the family circle.

Unfortunately, many young people are caught up in the emotional web surrounding their adoption. They, their birth parents, and their adoptive parents are unable to understand each other's problems and often conjure up distorted pictures warped by suspicion, envy, and fear.

FANTASIES

It is not uncommon for those who have been adopted to fantasize about "what could have been." It is easy to let your mind explore how it might have been different had you been living with your biological parents.

- *They* would have let me go on the trip.
- *She* wouldn't have been so strict.
- *They* would have liked my friends.
- *He* would have cared more.
- *She* would have loved me more.

Jennifer was six months old when she was adopted. She is now fifteen. While other girls her age fantasize about romance and what the future may be, Jennifer's thoughts are about something else. She thinks about her birth mother, wondering over and over how it would have felt to be held by her. What did she look like back then? What does she look like now? Did she cry when she had to give Jennifer away? What are her favorite foods? Even though her adoptive mother is caring and supportive, Jennifer can't help fantasizing about her birth mother.

When fantasies are conjured up about the biological parents, they are often along the lines of perfection, the ideal mother and father. The birth parents are thought of as handsome, beautiful, and kind. The idea is that one day they will come searching for their child. There will be a tearful reunion, and everyone will live happily ever after.

Milton Senn and Albert Solnit, in their textbook *Child Psychiatry*, say that "fantasies about birth parents are usually built from disguised impressions and wishes about the *adoptive parents* and have little to do with the birth parents per se."

I was told that my "real mother" was too young and too poor to keep me. Now I imagine that I show up at her door and we hug each other and cry. We talk for hours, making up for all the lost time.

Jeff is captain of the high school soccer team and is crazy about sports. He plays baseball in the summer, football in the fall, and coaches junior high students three afternoons a week at the local YMCA. Jeff's adoptive parents are business people. His dad is an accountant with a large company and his mother is a legal secretary.

I can't help but imagine that my "real dad" is a sports nut like myself. I picture him cheering in the stands for me, jumping up and down when I score a point. I think he plays football with a major team.

In truth, Jeff's biological father, Mark, is not interested in sports. He is in fact a big-city architect, very detail-oriented, engrossed in measurements and scale drawings. Mark creates blueprints for buildings. Jeff has created Mark for himself.

Common Fantasies

- My birth mother is a famous person.
- My birth father is a hero.
- I will find my real parents.
- My birth mother is wealthy.
- I have a beautiful sister somewhere.

Fantasy vs. Fact

It is easy to imagine what might have been, but it is important to distinguish fantasy from fact, to keep in tune with what is happening in the present. Try to see your everyday life as it is at the moment. Are things as bad as they seem? Think about it. Ask yourself these questions:

- Who takes care of me when I'm sick?
- Who attends my school functions?
- Who drives me to social events?
- Who prepares my meals?
- Who listens to my complaints?
- Who plans for my future?

Try to concentrate on what *is*. Putting your past in perspective will help you to go forward in the future.

FEARS

Many times young people who are living with adoptive parents have trouble establishing sound relationships. They fear getting close, letting down their guard and expressing how they really feel. They are hesitant to establish boy/girl relationships because they are afraid of being exposed, of having someone find out about their unknown past. Let's talk about some of those fears. See if they sound familiar.

Fear of Failure

- I'm not what they expected.
- I'm different from the rest.

- I'm not as smart.
- I'm not as good-looking.
- I'm not popular.

In my adoptive father's mind there is a picture of the perfect son. I know that I don't live up to his dream, and I know that he is disappointed. He tries to hide the fact, but it comes out in different ways, in his tone, in what he says, in his silence. I know he thinks he's failed as a father. His attitude has left an impression on me, a permanent feeling of failure.

Fear of Abandonment

- She'll leave me like my real mother did.
- They'll send me away.
- Since my real father deserted my mother, all men are bad.

Fear of Being Unloved

- I am not loved like a "blood child."
- I feel like the unwanted product of an affair.
- They are not really interested in me.
- They regret having adopted me.

Fear of Being Exposed

- I may have inherited a genetic disease.
- His parents will find out about my unknown past.
- What if I fall in love with a birth relative?
- My real past is a dark secret.

COMBATING NEGATIVE FEELINGS

Other feelings that often surface are those of being self-conscious, withdrawn, anxious, suspicious, and envious. These feelings surface most often during your adolescent years. Adolescence is a powerful, stressful time, regardless of parental status. Whether you are living with a single parent, adopted parents, or your grandparents, it is a time when these feelings arise. They may appear suddenly, out of the blue, or they may brew silently for weeks.

It is easier to blame a negative mood on the fact that you are adopted than to look into the real reason that the mood has surfaced.

For example, you have been brooding because your parents wouldn't let you go on the weekend ski trip with your friends. You haven't spoken a word in days, and you barely acknowledge anyone who tries to speak with you. "Why? Because I am adopted. My real parents would have let me go to the mountains. These people don't care. They don't care if I have a good time or not."

Stop for a moment. Take the words *Because I'm adopted* out of your vocabulary. Search for another possible reason why your parents will not let you go on the trip. Could it be because:

- The roads are closed because of an ice storm.
- There have been travelers' warnings for the area.
- The people you were to go with have been in trouble with the law.

When the fact that you are adopted is taken away from your reasoning in a situation, other explanations may come to light.

• • •

Karen was anxious about singing the lead in the Spring Musical at school. She felt that her parents had pushed her into it, that they were theater people and were trying to mold her into the child they had always wanted. "My real mom and dad would never make me do this; *they* would understand."

Karen has the idea that her birth mother would have acted and felt differently, that *because she is adopted* she is being asked to do something that makes her anxious and uneasy. If Karen would take the words *because I'm adopted* out of her reason for being nervous, other reasons would come to light.

- Karen is actually proud of her voice. It is the idea of a packed auditorium that gives her the jitters.
- She has not learned the words to the songs.
- Her boyfriend will be watching on opening night.

Anger

Understanding your anger and expressing it in a healthy manner is crucial to your relationship with your parents. When dealing with anger, ask yourself these questions:

1. What am I feeling? Is it anger? If it is, recognize it as such.
2. Where is my anger coming from? Identify the source.
3. What is happening to make me angry?
4. How can I deal with my anger?

Some possible answers to the fourth question:

a. Talk to the person who is making you angry.
b. Shift gears and listen.

c. Get someone to listen to you talk about your anger.

d. Work it off in some way: play tennis, jog, exercise.

Often you don't know yourself why you feel a certain way, or how you feel about a certain person. You experience feelings that are new and that you can't put into words. You may feel embarrassed and confused because you can't express these feelings. You don't understand them, and you don't want to admit to your parents that you can't confide in them or share your feelings and thoughts.

Besides negative feelings, you may have thoughts and opinions on drugs, sex, racial bias, or religion. Parents sometimes react very strongly when you don't confide in them. Although adolescence is a normal and natural time to begin to pull away and allow yourself space, delicate balancing must occur within the family circle.

Try to keep the lines of communication open: It is a difficult time for all, but hang in there, it will pass.

VALUES

In the process of sorting out your feelings, you may also be taking a closer look at who you really are.

- Am I right about this?
- Did I jump to a conclusion?
- Have I been acting hostile?
- Was I wrong to feel that way?

Rather than feeling definite about something, you may begin to feel uncomfortably neutral. You discover that many well-respected persons outside the family have values that differ from yours or those of your parents.

Until now, you have considered your parents' word infallible. Suddenly things seem different. You wonder whose values are the right ones. Were the things you were afraid to do in the past really wrong? That prompts you to examine your own values.

Assessing Values

Are these values really yours, or are they borrowed without change to please your parents? If you cannot find an answer, you may be afraid to move in any direction. You no longer consider your parents' values as absolute, but you have found no substitutes of your own. This may make you depressed and uncertain about your future.

During this time you may feel impelled to drop out of school to spend time contemplating, or traveling. You may decide to take an "unchallenging" job while trying to find yourself. *There is hope.* After a time, most of you who have gone through this period of growth find that much of what you thought was dull and pointless takes on new meaning and importance. School becomes a more meaningful part of your plan for the future, a future that you believe is *your own*, not one conceived by your parents.

SUMMARY

In this chapter, we have heard from others how it feels to be adopted. Perhaps you have identified with some of the feelings and situations described.

Being adopted has different meanings to different people. To those of you struggling with day-to-day conflicts it is a tough time, a time of reevaluating yourself and your position in your adoptive family. It is a time of wondering "what might have been" and what the future will bring. It is a time of assessing values.

It is important, above all, to *value yourself*. Realize that you are a physical, emotional, rational, and social being, like all other human creatures in the universe. Have a sense of yourself as a person and of your individual strengths and weaknesses. Understand that your problems are similar to others, often in the same situations.

Try to keep in mind that your adoptive parents *are* your real parents, the ones who bring you up, who take care of you, and see that you are well and happy. They are the ones who love you day after day and help you to grow into a good and responsible person.

Most important, appreciate your *family ties*. They are based far more on love, caring, and nurturing than on bloodlines.

CHAPTER 2

Handling Upsetting Remarks

Gloria knows that kids can be cruel. She only has to look as far as her eight-year-old son, Scott. Every afternoon she consoles him about taunts and jeers from his classmates. And for what reason? Simply because he can't play ball as well as the other boys. He strikes out most of the time and fumbles catches. Actually, Scott reads better than the rest. He's smart, and generally a happy kid. But because he is somewhat behind in physical coordination, the other boys tease him and call him names. "You're a bad player!" "You're clumsy!" "You throw like a girl!" "You lost our game!"

And how does Scott react to the remarks? Like an eight-year-old. "I am not!" "You're stupid, I'm going to punch you!" He reacts with hurt and anger, often taking it out on his younger sister at home. As he grows older and begins to reach adolescence, his way of striking back should change. For one thing, he will be more mature physically. And who knows? Maybe he'll end up a star player, and *they* will be asking to play on *his* team. In any event, as he reaches young adulthood, he will handle upsetting comments in a more mature manner.

No doubt the remarks will still sting. Negative comments hurt. They hurt all through our adult life. It's the way we respond to them that changes as we mature. At eight, you can sputter back an insult with tears in your eyes. At eighteen, you should be able to hear it and deal with it either by ignoring it, responding in a direct/honest approach, or correcting the speaker if he or she is wrong.

As you probably know, many adults cannot handle cutting remarks or insults. Some of them resort to childlike behavior and strike out at the insulting person. How often have you seen an adult lose control and berate someone who has made a negative remark? He/she sees red and wants to hurt the person back. Sometimes just offhand remarks can make people see themselves in a different light:

- You seem to be putting on a little weight.
- Really? I thought you were older than that.
- Changing jobs again?
- You really should learn to cook.
- Oh, you're just a housewife; you don't work?
- Are those lines I see around your eyes?
- *What* did you do to your hair?

Some adults can laugh off a negative comment and go their way. Others react differently, running to the mirror. Do I really look older? Have I put on weight? Am I getting wrinkles? Often, just a simple remark about your physical self can put you into a state of worry or depression. Oh, so that's what everyone thinks of me. I'll never make another meal. I'm changing my hair back to its old style. Negative remarks made about our*selves* can be upsetting, whatever our age.

How many of you remember cruel remarks that were made to you back in your earlier years of school? Were you a "fatso"? Did they call you "ugly" or "short stuff"? Did they make fun of the clothes you wore or the way you spoke?

How did you respond? Remarks made about your physical self are tough enough to handle. But those of you who are adopted have had to handle other remarks as well: the never-ending comments about the fact that you are adopted. Perhaps they are the most hurtful comments of all. They are not knocking the braces on your teeth, or an extra ten pounds. They are challenging your parents, your past, and your place in society. Do any of these sound familiar?

- Your *real* mother didn't want you.
- My mom says you're an orphan.
- Your brother is not your *real* brother.
- What's it like to be adopted?

As you grew older, the questions still came. Now they were put in a little broader sense:

- Does it bother you, not knowing who you *really* are?
- How could your own mother give you away?
- Why doesn't your real mother try and find you?
- How do you know what you'll look like?

How do you respond to these questions? Most of them are made by well-meaning people. They are not said purposely to take a mean shot at you. The speakers often don't realize the impact of the remarks, which can be hurtful to you.

You may react with *anger* initially. You may want to strike out at the speaker. But try to remember that the person is probably misinformed about what adoption really is. To him/her, adoption may mean something different, perhaps something strange or secretive. S/he may feel sorry for you, even though you are happy and secure in your adoptive family.

It is important to *respond* and *relate* to such people. Show an interest in what they are thinking. Try to help them with any misconceptions they may have about adoption.

Sandra had to break the news to her friend Ann that her mother wouldn't let her go to the movies on Friday night. "That's not fair!" said Ann. "You should go anyway. *She's* not your real mother, you shouldn't have to listen to *her*."

Sandra knew how Ann felt about adoption. It had come out in comments she had made previously. To Ann, an adopted person was like a displaced person, taken in by a family on a temporary basis. Sandra did not criticize her friend. Instead, she identified Ann's feelings and acknowledged them. This is how Sandra replied:

> I *do* have to listen to her. She *is* my mother, the only mother I have ever known. It is my sister's birthday on Friday. We are having a party for her on Friday night. That is why I can't go with you.

In a few direct sentences, Sandra replied to how Ann felt. There were no harsh words, no insults directed at Ann. Sandra chose to use a *nonjudgmental reply*. She also began to teach Ann what adoption is all about. She included Ann in conversations that she had with her mother. She showed Ann pictures of herself when she was first brought home. She answered many of Ann's questions, some of which Ann was hesitant to ask for fear of sounding stupid. Sandra and Ann strengthened their friendship as the lines of communication were opened between them.

Sometimes a negative comment cannot be shrugged off or ignored. You cannot handle it with a simple reply. Your day was going smoothly. Everything seemed okay. You were happy, until your friend happened to comment: "You know, I was thinking. It's too bad you'll never know who your real parents are. It must be weird not knowing who you really are." And then you start thinking: He's right. I'll probably never know. They pity me. They feel sorry for me. And then you start feeling sorry for yourself. You find that you are consumed by these thoughts, and you are left in a depressed mood that can last for days, sometimes even weeks or longer.

Remarks like those, as well as others that you have probably heard, will in all likelihood come your way at various times throughout your life. Let's see how you might handle them now, so that future ones can be dealt with in a positive rather than a negative way. First, it is important to realize that the remarks are not new. You have probably heard them in the past. It shouldn't really shock you to hear someone refer to your adoption in a questionable way. Try to ask yourself these questions:

- Why is this person making this comment?
- Is s/he telling me something that I don't already know?

- Is s/he trying to hurt my feelings?
- Could s/he be just curious or possibly misinformed?
- What good would it do to react in anger?

Instead of reacting in anger, take a second to see why the person might be making the comment or asking the question.

Let's see how a comment made to Mark was handled.

Jeff: Doesn't it feel kind of strange?
Mark: What?
Jeff: You know, being adopted.
Mark: Why do you ask?
Jeff: Well, because for one thing, you don't look anything like your family. You don't even know what you'll look like when you get older.
Mark: Neither do you.
Jeff: But I can look at my parents. They both are tall and have blond hair.
Mark: Your sister is short and has red hair.
Jeff: Yes, but I still think it's strange.
Mark: It's okay. I understand how you feel.

Mark's attitude and his honest reply was enough to satisfy Jeff. Most often, a *nonevaluative* response (which Mark used) does not contain either praise or criticism. Instead, it identifies feelings and acknowledges opinions.

COPING WITH RELATIVES

As you probably know, not all grandparents, aunts, uncles, or cousins may be pleased with your adoption into the family. Maybe you have picked up some remarks that were made behind your back. Many adoptees have heard the comment at one time or another, "You know, sometimes we almost forget that you are adopted." How often have you felt that your relatives acted outwardly pleased but inwardly were not fully adjusted to your adoption? Some relatives view the adoption as something secretive that has happened in the family.

Usually, the stronger your emotional attachment to the relatives who make the remarks, the more difficult it is to ignore them. You live among these people and see them often. It is hard not to respond to them in some way.

Beth's adoptive uncle always treats her like a fragile doll. He hovers over her at family gatherings and makes uncalled-for remarks such as "Where would you be if it were not for us?" He sees himself as the doting, concerned uncle, but Beth sees him in a different light.

> My uncle makes me feel like I'm from a different planet. He singles me out at family dinners and actually gives me extra portions of food. He brings me expensive gifts, things that I never use. I tried telling him not to treat me like this, but it doesn't help. Now, I just ignore him. It's the only thing I can do.

Pam had a similar problem with an aunt. This is how she handled it.

> We have an aunt who visits us a few times a year. When she sees me, she has the habit of telling me how "lucky" I am to be adopted into the family. One time I took her aside and told her how I felt about her comment. She said that she never realized it bothered me. She apologized and never said it again.

All families are different. They are made up of people with different personalities. There is really no "right" way of answering relatives who make remarks about your adoption. You might choose to take them aside and explain how you feel, as Pam did. You might want to confront them and ask them *why* they feel the way they do about you.

> I just laugh at comments made by the outside family. Sometimes it works. They see how ridiculous they sound.

> My mom always talks for me. If someone says something about my being adopted, she talks to that person.

> I ask them why they are saying what they do. I throw the ball back to them.

A sense of humor, an honest reply, or simply ignoring the person are some ways of responding to family members. Can you think of some comments that have been made to you? How did you respond?

FAVORITISM

Another way that relatives can reveal their feelings is by showing favoritism toward birth children in the family. They may bring gifts to your brothers and sisters and ignore you, or give you a gift of lesser value. Many times they don't realize what they are doing. Take the case of Ted.

Ted is fifteen and of Korean descent. He was adopted by his American parents when he was two. Each year at

Christmas, Ted's adoptive grandmother gives presents to all three children in the family, but Ted's brother and sister receive much nicer gifts, an obvious show of favoritism. Ted's grandmother has always had difficulty accepting him into the family.

Ted is now aware of his grandmother's motivation. At first, he was hurt and resentful. He always thought that something was wrong with him, that he was bad in some way because of the way she treated him in comparison to his brother and sister.

As he grew older, however, Ted realized that his grandmother held a deep-rooted prejudice against people of other races and nationalities. This was something he could not change. He recognized the situation and chose to ignore her deliberate acts of favoritism. Now, on receiving a gift, he thanks her along with the others and goes his way. He has even begun to see humor in her actions, and secretly wonders each year what gift she will come up with for him.

When Ted recognized that the problem was with his grandmother and not himself, he was able to handle the situation in a mature way.

MOM LIKES YOU BEST!

Yet another common situation within the family unit encompasses the feelings of favoritism: the resentment felt by your brothers or sisters because you are the adopted one. Do the following comments sound familiar?

- You let Jan stay up and watch TV late because she's adopted.
- You love Jan more than me.
- You think Jan is the special one.

- Jan gets more privileges than we do because she's adopted.
- I wish I were adopted.

Sometimes brothers and sisters resent the fact that your place in the family circle might be seen in a different light than theirs. Perhaps they've heard your parents refer to you as "special" or "chosen." They see a need to challenge *their* position in your parents' eyes.

The "Mom likes you best" syndrome happens in all families, adoptive or biological. Jealousy and striving for parental attention exist when there is more than one child in the family. Even the simple gesture of giving one child an extra piece of candy or a bigger hug can start the wheels turning in the mind of the other child. "Dad prefers Lucy to me. He brings her more things. He gives her more attention. I can see it. He does not love me as much as he loves Lucy."

Can you imagine, then, how adoptive brothers or sisters can experience feelings of jealousy, especially when they pick up on words such as "special one" in regard to you? Perhaps your adoptive mother has put together a scrapbook for only you, reflecting the first days when you were brought home. Maybe you really are given that extra hug (unconsciously) by your dad. Your brothers or sisters cannot help but notice some underlying special attention in the way your parents treat you. And it sometimes comes out as a feeling that you are the favored one in the family. It becomes difficult for your brothers and sisters to love and accept you when it appears to them that you are singled out as being a little bit better than they are.

Sibling rivalry and jealousy are common in most families at one time or another. Sometimes the feelings disappear as the children reach adulthood. In some instances, though, the feelings remain and become a permanent force between sibling adults.

The feelings about an adopted sibling being favored usually disappear as the children grow and establish close relationships. If you are adopted into a family that already has biological children, everyone has to go through a period of adjustment. As you get older, the feelings of "You are more special than we" should dissolve. The sibling bond is a complex and powerful connection.

PREJUDICES

We have discussed some of the remarks and comments that are made by friends and relatives. But many of you may have had to deal with other remarks besides the ones regarding your adoption. These are the remarks about the fact that you are of a minority heritage or are physically handicapped. Do you fall into either or both of these categories? How often have you been the target of personal questions, or stares? What was your reaction?

Transracial Adoptees

People who make comments about your race or the fact that your parents are of a different "color" often do not stop to think how they are affecting you. They say whatever comes to their mind. It is extremely difficult for some people (particularly older people) to face their own latent (hidden) feelings of prejudice. Perhaps you have been subjected to the individual who goes up to your parents in a restaurant or other public place and comments about their adopting a black child.

Many people take the attitude that white children should be adopted into white families and black children into black families. Never mind that you are happy and being raised in a loving home by wonderful parents. Some people cannot see past "color." They simply say what they think.

In her book *Mixed Families*, Joyce Ladner talks about some of the attitudes that society has regarding transracial adoptions. She says that feelings run strong on both sides, that the black community often feels that a white family cannot give a black child the necessary psychological preparedness for future problems regarding his race. They ask whether she is being raised as a proper black child? Many people focus their attention on the transracial aspects of the adoption, rather than the adoption itself.

Racial attitudes still exist, and will for the foreseeable future. It is important to feel comfortable about your adoption regardless of your race. Try to project a positive attitude toward these people, even though your initial reaction to their stares and comments may be anger. Try to maintain a sense of humor. Your image of self-assurance will in all likelihood be matched by equal acceptance.

Handicapped Adoptees

We have seen how some people harbor feelings of prejudice against persons of other races, but society practices other kinds of prejudice. Do you know people who are prejudiced against those who are of a different religion? Or prejudiced against women who are divorced? Some young people are prejudiced against their peers who have more money or higher social status than they do.

Still another kind of prejudice is around, one that is not openly talked about but still practiced. It is prejudice against handicapped people. I'm sure those of you who are handicapped are aware of this. Have you at one time or another been the butt of a cruel joke? Have you been excluded from a club or organization by your classmates? Been overlooked for school projects or activities by your teacher? Perhaps you have been subjected to stares by adults and children. Although most people are kind and understanding of the disabled, there are still those few who make life difficult. Also hard to cope with are the over-sympathetic people such as:

- The teacher who counsels you out of her class because she feels it will be too demanding for you.
- The well-meaning person who sees your cane and grabs you by the arm to help you across the street, assuming that you are lost and need help.
- The classmate who plans a party and doesn't ask you to participate because she feels it will be too difficult for you.
- The English professor who excuses you from normal class requirements.

I'm sure you have your own list of all the things you've experienced. Most acts against the disabled are unintentional. It is important for you to *speak up* if you feel that you have been slighted. Say that you really would like to be included in the planning of the party. No one will know if you don't come forward on your own behalf. If you feel that your teacher is being too cautious or lenient with you, try to express your feelings.

- I know you are trying to help, but I feel that I can do this on my own.
- I feel that you are drawing unnecessary attention to me by excusing me from projects.
- Please let me decide what is too difficult.

- I appreciate your assistance, but I can get around by myself.

Try to show people that you are not seeking pity or sympathy, but simply the dignity of being *yourself*.

At times you may find yourself stared at by children. They may come up to you and ask:

- Why can't you walk?
- How does that chair work?
- Why do you wear that thing on your neck?
- What happened to you?

Try to remember that children are curious by nature. Often, just a simple, direct answer will satisfy them:

- I was born with cerebral palsy. These braces help me to walk.
- My legs are not as strong as yours. I use a wheelchair to get around. Would you like to see how it works?

Questions and remarks made by young children can be dealt with in a kind and informative manner. They don't really want a long, detailed explanation of why you get around on wheels instead of legs. They are usually satisfied with a short, friendly response. Questions asked by older people are sometimes more difficult to deal with.

- How long do you have to be in that chair?
- Will you always have to use crutches?
- What exactly is your diagnosis?
- Do you have to wear that neck brace all the time?

These questions are usually asked out of curiosity; they are not meant to pry or offend. Questions about your personal habits are a different matter. Some people will ask about your sleeping habits, or your bathing habits, or your personal hygiene. These questions need not be answered, especially if you find them offensive.

If a subject is one that you really don't care to talk about, *be honest.* Tell the questioner, "It's a personal matter. I don't care to talk about it." If it's a medical question and you feel like explaining, do so. Try to recognize the person's curiosity, but never feel that you have to divulge anything about yourself that you don't want to. Your success in relating to others will be affected by the way you understand and project your own handicap.

LET'S PRACTICE

We saw earlier how kids can be cruel and say things that hurt other kids. But some adults (as you well know) can be just as cruel without even realizing the impact of an offhand comment or remark. They may not mean to be upsetting, but we're all human, who wouldn't be upset? The point to remember is that their remarks are often made out of ignorance. Maybe they're curious. Maybe their grandparents always felt a certain way about adoption or about minorities. Either way, it's really how you respond that matters. Your initial reaction may be to strike out, or to cry, or insult the speaker. But that is how eight-year-old Scott would respond. What you should try to do is acknowledge the comment and take a second to figure out why the person is saying it. Then respond in a mature manner, using your sense of humor if need be.

- Okay, softball's not my game. But I challenge you to a race around the track.
- To me, she *is* my real mother. But I appreciate your concern.
- I know that my being a different color bothers you, but it doesn't matter to me or my family.
- These wheels are my legs. I wouldn't be able to get around without them.
- How do I bathe? That's really a personal matter. I don't care to discuss it.

Following are some guidelines designed to help you cope with remarks about your adoption, your race, or your disability.

- Try not to mention that you are adopted in every other sentence. It is an open invitation for others to do the same.
- Remember that negative comments made about your adoption often stem from a person's misconception and lack of information about the subject.
- Don't try to hide the fact that you are adopted. It is nothing to be ashamed of.
- Don't expect to be treated as special by others.
- If you are disabled, answer questions as honestly as you can. Never feel that you have to explain anything that you feel is personal.
- Try to keep a sense of humor.
- Realize that many people carry with them hidden feelings of prejudice. You alone cannot change the way a person feels.

SUMMARY

If I could stress just one important point in regard to
handling upsetting remarks, it would be this: The way you
respond will tell a person how you feel in half a second. If
you feel comfortable with yourself and are confident and
sincere in your answer, it will project to the speaker. We
all know that what we really think or would like to do and
what we actually do are two different things.

If my sister were to tell me that I could stand to lose a
few pounds, I'd really like to tell her off. I'd like to say,
"How dare you say that to me; I'm not that bad. What's a
few extra pounds?" But I wouldn't. I'd see that she is my
sister. She's a health nut. She's thin and she jogs, and to
her a few extra pounds are a big thing. I see where she's
coming from.

There are no laws or government agencies to protect our
emotions. We are all vulnerable to the negativism that
surrounds us. Some people can take it better than others.

You can meet negativism more easily by expressing your
feelings clearly and giving a definite impression of where
you stand. If an exceptionally disturbing comment happens
to come your way, try to hear the message of the speaker.
Make a concerned effort to see where that person might be
coming from. Then make your reply. And stick with it,
riding out whatever may follow. This calls for courage.
Your *belief* and your *behavior* stand behind your courage:
how you feel about yourself, and how you project those
feelings. It is important, above all, to be honest with
yourself and with others. Honesty forms a solid base upon
which all growth can take place.

CHAPTER ◇ 3

Who Am I?

In Chapter 2 we talked about upsetting remarks made
by well-meaning friends and relatives. We saw how
sometimes an innocent comment about yourself can
change the way you feel. But where do our feelings come
from? Why do we act and feel the way we do? Have you
ever wondered why you are sensitive to some remarks, yet
completely indifferent to others?

Let's explore the development process of *personality*:
why we act and think the way we do. Let's look at the
journey we take from childhood to young adulthood and
talk about the *search for identity* (finding oneself) along the
way.

For those of you who are adopted, one of the most
frustrating things to deal with is the desire to know more
about yourself but not being able to find out. You may ask
yourself questions such as: Am I from a good background?
Do I carry some genetic disease? Who can assure me that
I don't?

Did you ever stop and wonder why some things are difficult for some people, yet easy for others? Why can one

person be such a whiz at math, yet another of the same age have to struggle with it?

No one in Jane's adoptive family had musical ability, but she learned to play the piano at an unusually early age. She liked to play for hours, and always wondered why it seemed so natural to her. As she grew older, she suspected that she had inherited the talent. She eventually discovered that her birth grandmother was a concert pianist.

THE SEARCH

To find out more about yourself, you must first develop a *sense* of who you really are. This often grows out of your childhood experiences and your attempts to make sense out of the things that have happened to you along the way. It also affects the way your parents, your friends, and others react to your personality. Some experiences that occurred in your first years of school have traveled with you into young adulthood. They are a big influence in the way you act and feel at the present time.

In a physical sense, you can easily look into the mirror and comment on your reflection.

- I am blonde.
- I have brown eyes.
- I am short.
- I have freckles.

But where do you look when you want to dig deeper than the physical? How do you answer:

- Why I feel comfortable in the company of certain types of people.
- Why I like music, but not art.

- Why I love cats, but shy away from dogs.
- Why I feel uneasy in crowded places.
- Why red is my favorite color.

Let's look at how the components of your personality combine to form the *real you*.

Patti was eight years old when she first experienced death. Her parakeet was crushed by accident in the doorway of her bedroom.

I remember seeing the bird fly out of the cage and across my room as it did so many times before. My mother walked in and closed the door behind her. At the exact moment before the door closed, the bird decided to fly into the next room. It flew into the doorway and got caught when the door closed. I remember seeing the bird lying on the floor. A cold chill went through me. It's hard to explain. I could not pick it up. I could not touch it. Now, ten years later, I still do not feel comfortable in the presence of any bird. Even going into a pet store makes me uneasy. That feeling has stayed with me all these years.

As you can see, a bit of Patti's past has traveled with her, combining with her present and helping to shape her personality as it is today. Whether it was the loss of her pet, or experiencing death in that particular way, a definite *feeling* (about birds) was formed at that time.

The same can be true of the different *moods* that you experience, the way you act and react about certain events or certain people. Can you find yourself in some of the descriptions below?

- I am talkative.
- I am a leader.
- I am confident.
- I am energetic.
- I am shy.
- I am quiet.
- I am a follower.
- I am a slow mover.

Rick is living with his second set of foster parents in five years. His first set took him in when he was nine. They were strict, overbearing people and did not want to admit that they had made a mistake in asking to take in a child. They knew little about raising children and did not know how to handle Rick. They kept him alone with them most of the time, isolated from other children his age. Rick developed few outside friendships and gradually became quiet and withdrawn.

When he was thirteen, Rick was sent to live with another family. Although his new foster parents made an honest effort to make Rick feel loved and welcome in their home, they could not break through the wall that he had built around himself. They soon gave up trying to bring him out and began to ignore his quiet ways. They felt that he was self-centered and living in "his own world." Eventually Rick totally stopped communicating with his family. He retreated even further. He did what was expected of him, but gave nothing of himself in return.

My relationship with myself is an unhappy one. I am moody. I pretend a lot when I'm with people. If I'm with someone who is up, I pretend to be up. When I'm with someone who is depressed, I am depressed. I am an imitation.

Much of Rick's present personality was taking shape while he was living with his first foster parents. He was left out socially at that time, and during the following years he added feelings of rejection and self-doubt to his emerging personality. Today, others view him as shy or arrogant, but Rick uses *withdrawal* as a major defense against his negative feelings.

Does this mean that all of your past experiences will present themselves in the future as the foundation of your personality? Not quite. Bits and pieces from your past find their way into your present self, making you think and act the way you do. It is how you emerge from childhood into adulthood as a *whole* that shapes your image.

Let's take a look at Bill, the way he describes himself at ten and sixteen, and what he is like today.

At ten	*At sixteen*
• I have one best friend.	• I am a loner.
• I do not like math.	• I am failing math.
• I like to write stories.	• I work on the newspaper.
• I do not like many foods.	• I am a picky eater.
• I sing in the choir.	• I play the guitar.

Bill went on to become an attorney. He married in his thirties and is the father of two children. Bill is on the thin side and still considers himself picky about food. He still has trouble with figures and avoids math at all opportunities. He enjoys music and writing short stories and articles in his free time.

As you can see, the combination of Bill's past and present self have helped create the person that he is today.

LOOKING BACK

Think back to your earlier years. Did you grow up on a ranch or in a home with a large area where you could run and ride your bike? Were you surrounded by pets: dogs, cats, rabbits? If you were happy and content in your environment as a young child, perhaps that is the kind of environment that you are seeking today. Try to remember things that made you feel good. Did you like working with your hands, building things out of clay or mud? Do you enjoy working with your hands now, such as putting together models or working on art projects?

Many people find that as they grow older they are stuck working in jobs where they are unhappy. They stay in the same place for a long time. Then, many years later, they begin to question *why* they are unhappy doing what they are doing. They may begin to explore things in their past and find they they grew up as a completely different type of person. Some may always have been shy and nervous speaking in front of people, yet find themselves struggling along in a sales job that often requires them to speak in public. By exploring certain aspects of your past, you may bring to light why you feel the way you do at the present time.

MOVING AHEAD

As you move toward adulthood, you face new expectations. You meet new responsibilities and experience a beginning drive for independence from your parents. A process of *internalization of identity* is taking place. You are sifting and sorting out feelings about what is okay and what is not okay in your life. It is a process of tearing down the old familiar self and rebuilding it into a new self.

Gone are fears of monsters in the dark. Enter new fears of getting a job, of passing a college entrance exam. Gone are giggles and schoolyard flirtations. Enter new sexual energies and desires. Changes take place in your intellect and in your social status. These changes come to everyone. They are unavoidable. You must try to meet them and come to grips with them in one way or another or you will be caught between childhood and adulthood.

Changes

Sometimes young adults get "stuck" in their childhood phase, feeling safe and secure in their environment. They become afraid to move forward and feel more comfortable acting years younger than they actually are. Below are some comments that you might have heard:

- She doesn't act her age.
- Why don't you grow up?
- It's time to cut the apron strings.
- He's still a mama's boy.
- Open your eyes and face the world.
- Stop being so immature.

I feel as if I will remain a child forever. I rely on my parents for everything. I don't feel that I can do anything on my own, yet I really do want to make the break. What's the matter with me? Why am I so afraid?

Shelley, 15

In the early teens it is understandable that you might want to put off or avoid thinking about the future and new responsibilities. It seems easier to focus on more immediate things, such as music or partying. But when you begin using the delay as a *defense mechanism* to avoid anxieties about the future, you get caught. You become unable to advance into young adulthood.

Perhaps you have experienced the same feeling that Shelley has. Have you wanted to begin breaking away from the security of your family and exploring the outside world? What stopped you? Do the following sound familiar?

- I want the job, but I'm afraid to go to the interview.
- I want to go to camp, but it's two weeks sleeping away from home.
- My parents are leaving on a trip, and I'm a nervous wreck.
- I was asked to join a club but I declined.

You begin to question where you *fit in*. The party you are at is filled with friends from your school. The atmosphere is lively, and everyone is having a good time. Except you. Even though you are surrounded by people, you feel lonely, out of place. You smile, but you wish you were at home watching TV.

Separation Anxiety

The feeling of having difficulty breaking away from a safe and secure pattern is described by psychologists as *separation anxiety*. It does not apply only to young adults; it is experienced in all age groups:

- The toddler left behind with a new baby-sitter.
- The husband leaving his family for an extended business trip.

- The mother leaving her child on the first day of kindergarten.

The anxiety is felt by both sides in any age group. It is important to realize that many others are experiencing the same doubts and feelings that you are. The maturation process does not automatically jump from childhood into adulthood. Some people make the transition smoothly and with few problems, but they are the exception rather than the rule. Most people move forward in some areas and stay behind longer in others. Some are secure in making lasting relationships but find that they put off anything that has to do with a commitment to work. If you see yourself caught with childlike insecurities in a rapidly changing adult body, try to remember that you are still in motion. You are moving along at your own pace, developing new concepts and ideas along the way.

The Group for Advancement of Psychiatry has suggested six criteria for determining when you have finally reached adolescence. They pinpoint the areas of greatest importance:*

1. Attaining separation and independence from parents.
2. Establishing sexual identity.
3. Making a commitment to work.
4. Developing a capacity for lasting relationships.
5. Developing a personal moral value system.
6. Making an emotional return to parents based on relative equality.

---

*The Family Handbook of Adolescence. John E. Schowalter, M.D., and Walter R. Anyan, M.D.

Jay at seventeen has been involved in a serious relationship with a girl for two years. His relationship with his parents has improved greatly, overcoming past years of turbulent conflict. Jay's problem lies in his commitment to work. He seem unable to hold a job for more than a few weeks at a time. He has had many opportunities for after-school employment, but he cannot bring himself to stay in any one position.

Jay's problem with work goes back to his earlier years. His parents always gave him generous amounts of spending money. They bailed him out of troublesome situations and never gave him the opportunity to stand up for himself. He was never taught the value of money and therefore came to expect assistance whenever things did not go as he wanted. When he became bored with a job he walked away, counting on his parents to help him out until the next job came along. To those who know Jay, he appears to be a mature individual, ready to tackle the world. He is, however, still caught in some of his childhood ways.

FINDING FAULT

Jay was not aware that he was immature in his commitment to work. But some of you may know where you are at the present time. You may feel that you are insecure in developing relationships, but that you have high moral standards of right and wrong.

You may not be ready to move forward, to try out a new experience. You may want to blame someone else for pushing you ahead into the adult world. You don't know exactly whom to strike out at for the push to move you toward increased responsibilities, so you blame your parents. Conflicts then arise in the family, and life becomes a series of irritations. The whole world begins to take on a negative aspect. Does this sound familiar?

- My parents don't trust me.
- I'm a loser.
- Who would want to date me?
- This house is a dump.
- I'll never get a job.
- School is a drag.
- My teachers don't like me.

You blame your adoptive parents because they can't answer many of the questions you have about your earlier years. At the same time, however, your parents may feel that *you* are to blame for the way you are acting and feeling at this time. They may feel that your negative thoughts are *deliberate* against *them*.

Seth and his parents had been fighting on and off for two years. His parents were sure that Seth was deliberately trying to destroy whatever relationship was left in the family. Seth's mother explained: "We enjoy a quiet environment/Seth picks fights with neighbors, bullies children, and teases dogs. We enjoy reading good literature/Seth clutters the house with comic books. We stress physical health/Seth refuses to do any type of exercize or eat the right foods.

As you can see, Seth's parents felt that he was doing everything he could to be the *opposite* of what they expected of him. Actually, Seth is in the process of emerging from his childhood ways into adulthood. He is moving toward independence from his parents and other adults and is feeling *personal power* (physical and intellectual). This is combined with a natural tendency to throw off adult authority.

In this time of change, Seth was becoming resentful of his parents. He saw them as undermining his feelings of self-worth and self-confidence.

Months later, however, his feelings about his parents began to change. He began to realize all that his parents had done for him throughout his life. He saw his father as well-meaning and doting, his mother as warm and trusting. It was at this time that Seth became increasingly independent and courageous in moving away from their protective wing and into situations in which he was on his own. He was in the process of finding his own sense of identity, emerging into his new adult self.

THE IMPORTANCE OF FRIENDS

As you move toward adulthood, another change will occur: the importance of *peer relationships*. We all get much of our feelings of self-esteem, our positive or negative identities, from the reactions of others to us. As you grow older, it is mainly your relationship with friends that influences your feelings about yourself. This is a major shift, and a very powerful one.

Some of you may find that you are happiest when surrounded by many friends, that you enjoy traveling in a group or clique. You make decisions among yourselves and form a special bond. In the past, you used to go to your parents for answers to issues; now, your friends become your main source of information on right and wrong.

Others of you may prefer the company of one friend, rather than a group. There may be one person with whom you prefer to share your views, someone who enjoys many of the same things that you do.

Debbie was asked to join many clubs and organizations at school. She did not feel comfortable in the company of many people, but she enjoyed being with Lori, her best friend since grade school. Lori and Debbie were like sisters. They shared secrets and stuck together throughout the school years. Debbie went to Lori about problems with boys and with parents, rather than discussing them with a group of friends. Many called Debbie a loner because she did not travel in a crowd. But she was comfortable with herself and her choice of one good friend.

Do you see yourself in Debbie? Or are you the type who feels comfortable in a group of friends? Whatever your choice, it is important for you to feel accepted by someone your age. When you were younger you may have received positive input about yourself from adults: a pat on the back for a job well done, or praise for something you accomplished. But now you look to your friends for building self-confidence and self-liking. To be liked by other people your age becomes one of the most important goals in life.

> You can't be too different or you're out. You have to be cool, but not too cool. You just walk the middle line and hope that you're considered "in" with those that count.
>
> Jeremy, 16

Although the major source of feelings during this time is the degree of acceptance and approval of your friends, some other figures may influence the way you feel: movie stars, rock stars, athletes, glamorous heroes. Have you ever patterned your hairstyle or your music style after someone famous? For some, *antiheroes* such as gang leaders may become important influences.

POSITIVE SELF-IMAGE

As we have seen, friendships play a major role in your journey toward adulthood. They help you to develop a positive self-image. Other factors that may also help you feel good about yourself are pride, a feeling of worthiness, self-confidence, self-respect, a good body image, and inner security.

At times it may seem impossible to feel good about yourself when everything in your life is going wrong. How can you feel worthy, when you are failing subjects in school? How can you feel self-confident, when you are an "outcast" socially? How can you project a good body image, when you are shorter than the rest and overweight? How can you have self-respect, when you are constantly told that you will never amount to anything?

It is difficult to ignore negative feedback and come out shining and feeling happy about yourself. It takes courage to try to overcome obstacles that are set in your way. To meet rejection, deal wih it, and continue on your way takes more courage than giving in to it.

Many successful actors and business people who have achieved fame and fortune came from backgrounds completely different from the lives they are living today.

Take the case of a well-known recording star whose records sell millions. She lives in luxury and travels in style. And most important, she is happy and content with her life as it is. That was not always the case. She grew up in a backwoods mining town, with few possessions to call her own. Others made fun of the way she dressed. But she had a knack for composing songs and a beautiful voice. She ignored her rundown environment and concentrated on the talent that she carried within her. She practiced singing and continued writing music. Eventually, people began to take notice. They saw that she had a special gift. They also saw her confidence and the proud way that she carried herself. She climbed the ladder of success after many years of hard work, achieving success by believing in herself, despite the odds against her.

This does not pertain only to superstars or celebrities. Think about some people that you have seen going that extra mile to achieve what they set out to get.

- The man in a wheelchair who attends college and is preparing for another four years in law school.
- The obese woman who diets faithfully for almost a year, finally reaching her goal loss of 80 pounds.
- The young boy from a poor family who works everyday after school, saving money for his future education.

Think about it. What are some obstacles that you feel might be blocking your way?

- Lack of money
- Explosive temper
- Physical handicap
- Conflict with parents
- Shy personality
- Problems with reading
- Low self-esteem
- Jealous nature

• Fear of failure
• Emotional instability

It is important to note that these obstacles are not permanent fixtures in your life. They can be met with, worked around, and eventually resolved. It will not happen overnight. You will not wake up one morning two hundred dollars richer, twenty pounds lighter, and feeling wonderful about yourself. But if you consciously work hard at making one thing right in your life, such as overcoming your jealousy, or reaching out socially to other people, you will notice a change over time. Maybe it's time to hire a tutor to help with your reading problems. Maybe it's time to take the wheelchair to the shopping center and get out among people.

Remember Patti's fear of birds? Rick's withdrawal from people? Shelley's fear of breaking away? What could these people do to overcome the negative feelings standing in their way? When you project positive feelings about yourself, others cannot help but pick up those feelings too. Pride, self-confidence, and inner security are all things that you alone can achieve. It does not take status or money to achieve them. All it takes is the desire to start moving forward in the right direction.

SUMMARY

In this chapter, we have talked about how personalities develop, about looking into your past to find explanations for some of the ways that you act or feel. It is important to remember that although you may have carried with you certain feelings from childhood, and those feelings are now standing in your way, they can be worked with and changed. They do not have to be permanent blocks in your path to success.

We also discussed how a person establishes a sense of identity. We learned that as you receive all the input from the world, internalize it, and accept it as real, certain feelings of identity develop. These feelings become yardsticks for evaluating your actions, for making decisions, and for judging what is right and wrong.

Yes, it may be frustrating not being able to know what kind of blood you carry, or how tall you may grow, or how old you were when you first smiled. But you do have the answers to your childhood in the *feelings* and *memories* of things that only *you* experienced.

The search for identity does not end when you reach your eighteenth birthday. It continues for the rest of your life. Many men and women in their 40's, 50's, and 60's are changing careers. Some are returning to school. They are asking themselves the same questions that you are asking yourself now: Who am I? Where do I fit in? What makes me do the things that I do? The search is a continual process. It is a process of experiencing triumphs and reaching out for new dreams. Discovering yourself can be a new and exciting experience.

CHAPTER ◇ 4

Coping with Conflict

onflict. What is it, exactly? What brings it about?
The dictionary defines it as battle, disagreement,
opposition, antagonistic state.

Many of you who are currently involved in conflict
would probably describe it in much broader terms. Maybe
you would describe it as an emotional confrontation that
involves verbal accusations or physical or emotional abuse.
You might describe it as a problem with authority, such as
the inability to get along with your teacher or someone
whose rules you must abide by. People have their own
definitions of conflict as they see it or are living with it. The
fact is that conflict exists when there are opposing ideas,
when there are differences of opinion.

If you say you think it will rain, and your brother says he
thinks it will be clear and sunny, you have conflicting ideas
about the weather. Let's say it stays sunny. He is right.
You concede. End of conflict.

What if you didn't concede? What if you decided to hold
a grudge against your brother, not because it stayed sunny,
but because he was right and you were wrong. You

couldn't stand it. From then on, if he said black, you said white. If he said cold, you said hot. Your relationship was reduced to one conflict after another. That is how it is for some people.

Maybe you are living with the everyday squabbles of having to follow the rules of your house. Or the bickerings over your desire for an increase in your allowance. If so, you're lucky. Many others would like to be in your shoes. Chances are that you have worked out past problems and now have an open line of communication with your friends and family.

This chapter is for those who are experiencing a different kind of conflict, the kind that affects happiness and the sense of well-being. This conflict could be the kind that seriously damages your relationship with members of your adoptive family and with friends as well. These are not disagreements about the weather. They are daily battles that may continue through adulthood if not resolved.

The accompanying chart shows some common areas of conflict, some possible causes, and what might be done to try to solve them. It also shows some possible results once the conflict is resolved. Study the chart. Can you add any of your own ideas to the columns? You might find yourself hidden somewhere in there. Try playing around with different combinations to fit your own situation. Mix and match the kinds and causes of conflict, then pick an alternative and see if you think it might work for you.

Maybe you are having problems with a teacher. You've probably heard the phrase "personality conflict." You feel that she doesn't like you for some reason and therefore is overly critical of your work. She criticizes you in front of the class, which makes you angry and upset. You, in turn, do not do the required assignments for her class. You feel, "What's the use? She doesn't like anything I do anyway."

So you do not make an effort in your work, which makes her even more angry. The two of you are embroiled in a conflict. What could possibly be done to work it out?

Let's examine some of the conflicts and see how others have been able to work them out. Their problems may be similar to the ones that you are experiencing; perhaps their solutions could work for you.

The first and most common feeling that is a source of conflict is *parental lack of caring*.

Kinds of Conflict	Causes of Conflict	Negative Results of Conflict	Possible Alternatives	Possible Outcome
Stepparent quarrels	High parental expecta-	Drug or alcohol	Admitting hostile	A feeling of belonging
Brother/sister arguments	tions	abuse	feelings	Ability to love uncondi-
Family	Feelings of lack of	Withdrawal from family	Opening up lines of	tionally
financial	emotional	or friends	communi-	Increased
problems	support	Running away	cation	mutual
Parents'	Lack of	Low self-	Getting	feelings of
marital	privacy	esteem	profes-	trust and
disputes	Feelings of	Inability to	sional help	respect
Abuse by a	being	relate to	Adopting	Development
family	manip-	others	new values	of stronger
member	ulated	Negative	Reconstruct-	family ties
Teacher/	Excessive	outlook on	ing	Establishment
student	criticism	life	priorities	of solid
conflict	Poor	Development	Compro-	relation-
Boyfriend/	communi-	of abusive	mising	ships
girlfriend	cation	nature	Realizing	Becoming a
arguments	Lack of time		what is	person in
Problem with	spent		really	your own
authority	Jealousy		important	right
figures				Feelings of
				self-worth
				and self-
				confidence

PARENTAL LACK OF INTEREST

Many changes in family life-styles have occurred in recent years. The growing incidence of divorce and the impact of inflation have contributed to the rise of two-career families. Parents have less time to spend with their kids than they did a generation ago. As a result, many young people today feel a loss of support, a lack of caring from their family.

This kind of family has few guidelines to follow. The attitude is one of "being able to do your own thing." While that may sound like a pretty good way of life to some, quite a few young people find it difficult to fit into this type of family unit. They feel that their parents are involved with their own problems and can't see beyond their own needs.

- He's too busy to take an interest in me.
- She doesn't listen to my problems.
- They never ask about school or my friends.
- They listen but don't *hear* me.
- I have to make an appointment to talk to them.
- My needs are last on their list.

Tina was seventeen. She was adopted when she was six. She had always had a secure and loving relationship with her adoptive parents until they divorced two years ago. At that time Tina's mother had to return to work and had little time to spend with her daughter. Tina felt that her mother had lost all interest in her, that she had become totally involved in her career and her own happiness. Whatever Tina said or did was met with indifference.

"I try to tell Mom something important and she says, 'Don't worry, it's nothing.' She doesn't take anything seriously. She acts as if nothing matters. She watches TV immediately after dinner until it's time for bed. I try to tell her what's on my mind, but she doesn't even look at me when I'm talking."

Tina felt that the major problem was that she was adopted, that if she were a "real" daughter, her mother would care about her problems. In her mind, Tina felt that her mother had lost interest in her because there was no blood connection between them. Tina began rebelling in various ways, all of which were a subconscious effort to get her mother's attention. These are some of things she did.

- Stayed out late with friends without calling home.
- Shoplifted small store items.
- Allowed her grades to fall off.
- Took money from her mother's purse and helped herself to her mother's makeup and jewelry.

Her mother, of course, reacted in anger, and a bitter conflict began brewing between them. They were fast losing touch with each other and each other's feelings. During this time of conflict, Tina felt the need for acceptance and approval in her life, which her mother was not fulfilling.

As we saw at the beginning of this chapter, there is always a conflicting side to the problem. Let's look at Tina's mother's side and see how she views the situation.

Tina's mother had devoted much of her earlier years to staying at home and taking care of her daughter. The two were very close and developed a sound and trusting relationship. After the divorce, however, she was forced to return to work. She was attempting to build a life for herself and her daughter and to secure a future for them both. Her main concerns were not to have to depend on her ex-husband for money, and to be able to save for Tina's education. To this end she had to work long hours, often not getting home until late in the evening. Because of this, she had to give up time spent with her daughter.

In her mind, Tina's mother felt that the conflict was because she was Tina's *adoptive mother*. Perhaps, she thought, Tina's "real" mother would have done better for her. She would not have failed. Tina would have been proud of her.

As you can see, the two had conflicting ideas as to why their relationship was deteriorating, but *adoption* was the first concern of both. Actually, they were going through a period of adjustment in their lives, as most families (biological or adoptive) do after a divorce—a major event that alters the family structure.

Tina began to consider her situation hopeless. These were her obstacles as she saw them:

- Blocked communication
- Loss of self-esteem
- Frequent depression
- Loss of relationship

Seeing no solution to her problem, Tina decided to seek advice from someone outside. She made an appointment with her school counselor. The counselor suggested that she take a new approach and proposed five things for her to do:

1. Sit beside your mother while she is watching TV. Share your thoughts on the program that you are watching.
2. Do something to surprise her, like having dinner ready when she comes home.

3. Take her to a movie. Try telling her some of the things that are on your mind when you are out of the house together.
4. Don't unburden yourself of everything at one time. Start with what you feel is most important.
5. Ask her about her problems, her worries.

It didn't work overnight, but it did work eventually. The wall between them was gradually broken down. What Tina perceived as lack of interest or lack of concern was in reality lack of time and lack of energy.

Think about it. Do you feel that someone close to you has little or no interest in what you say or do? Ask yourself these questions:

• What small gesture can I make to open the way to better communication?
• Is my problem important enough for an immediate interruption? Can it wait for another time?
• Does the fact that I'm adopted really have anything to do with the conflict?
• Is it lack of interest, or could it be lack of time or energy?

Remember that it takes time to reconnect a relationship that has come apart. But you may find that it grows stronger and closer after your problems have been talked through and worked out.

One important point should be mentioned. A small percentage of young people really are being raised by parents who do not care. These kids have complete freedom to do what they want whenever they want. If you find yourself in such a situation, try to *set your own restrictions*. *Learn to say no to yourself.* Try to set your own values and stick to them. It may not seem important now, but you'll be glad you did when you look back on this time.

LACK OF PRIVACY

Everyone has a right to privacy. We all need some space, some time, and an opportunity for a separate and private existence. What are some of the ways in which you think people invade your privacy?

- Asking personal questions?
- Entering your room without permission?
- Listening in on your phone conversations?
- Opening your mail?
- Discussing your personal life with others?

Daniel's privacy is invaded every day after school. His mother meets him at the door with a list of questions. How was school? Who did you eat lunch with? What did you do in science class? Where did you buy that sweater? How much did you pay for it? Are you going to call Mary today?

Daniel walks past her, goes straight upstairs to his room, and closes the door. He stays there until dinner time. Unfortunately, the questions start again. Who are you going to ask to the dance? Where are you going this evening? Who were you talking to on the phone before?

Daniel's hostile feelings toward his mother grow by the day. He often ends up exploding in the middle of dinner and leaving the house. His mother reacts by brooding, upset by his outbursts. This, in turn, makes Daniel feel guilty. Their conflict grows by the day. Their relationship is falling apart, almost to the point of no return. Or so it seems. But before we examine how Daniel tried to solve his problem, let's see how Andrew survived. Same problem, different circumstances.

Andrew is thirteen, recently adopted into a family with two biological sons, seven and nine. His privacy problem is due to invasion of his *physical space.*

When Andrew came to live with his adoptive family, he was given his own room. His two brothers began to enter his room whenever Andrew was out and go through his clothes, gadgets, and personal belongings. The younger boys felt that since Andrew was adopted, he was not their *real* brother and therefore he had no *real* rights in the family. They took advantage of him, which created a conflict between all the brothers.

Daniel's and Andrew's problems were similar, in that they were unable to cope with conflicts arising out of the invasion of their privacy by other family members.

What to Do

If you were to advise Daniel on how to solve his problem with his mother's questions, what would you say? Scream? Ignore her? Walk away? Insult her? Would any of those behaviors solve the conflict between them? Probably not. What about *compromising?* What if Daniel sat down with his mother and explained to her that in the future he would answer certain questions that she asked, but not all questions. He would answer questions about where he was going, with whom, and what time he would be back. All other questions, such as who was on the phone or whom he had lunch with were off-limits questions that did not have to be answered.

Daniel chose to compromise and answer only those questions that he felt were fair. His mother agreed, and over a period of time their conflict was resolved. He did not explode in anger and run out of the house. His mother knew that she would be met with a nonresponse to unfair questions, so she limited herself to what Daniel considered fair. Daniel eventually regained his privacy and his relationship with his mother by using compromise.

Would this also work in Andrew's case? What if Andrew sat down and explained to his younger brothers that he did not appreciate their snooping in his room when he was away. This might not work because of one important fact: What Andrew appreciated and what he didn't appreciate were of no concern to his brothers. To them, Andrew did not really count in the family. They saw him as less than equal because he was adopted.

Andrew devised his own plan. He began entering his brothers' rooms when *they* were away and helping himself to their things. He made it obvious that he had been invading their territory, which angered and upset them. They went to their parents, and the conflict was brought out in a family meeting.

When the parents heard how the boys really felt about Andrew's adoption, they realized that the *real* problem began there. They explained to the younger boys that Andrew had no more and no less status than they, that all three boys were equal in the family. The fact that Andrew was adopted had no bearing on what rights he had or what love was distributed. All three boys were considered the same in their parents' eyes.

Andrew agreed not to enter the boys' rooms when they were not around and not to take things that didn't belong to him, if they would agree to the same. Andrew's brothers accepted the compromise. Their conflict over territorial dispute was resolved. Besides compromising, Andrew and his family chose to open the lines of communication among all family members.

HIGH PARENTAL EXPECTATIONS

Some of you may have problems attempting to live up to your parents' dreams and expectations. No matter how hard you try, you feel that you are not good enough in their eyes. Perhaps you feel that your parents' love has become conditional on your achievement.

Because you are adopted, you may feel that you have to project an image of the child you feel they have always wanted—a type of child that you are not, but are trying to be. You may feel like a failure in your parents' eyes.

Sometimes a family that is strongly oriented toward academic accomplishments finds it difficult to accept a child who is not doing well in school.

If you see yourself in any of the above, it is important that you try to express your feelings of being inadequate to your parents. You may feel "stupid" or "funny" doing this, but often the parents do not realize how they are making the child feel. It is clearly unintentional.

Such acts or feelings may have originated when you were much younger, perhaps not long after you were brought home. Parents have a habit of comparing their children to other children.

- Oh, your baby is walking at eleven months? Mine is still crawling.
- My little girl can count to ten. Can yours?
- He's reciting the alphabet? I'll have to practice with Jill.

Unfortunately, as you grow older, you are still being compared. Many parents don't actually say it, but they may be thinking:

- His son is an A student. I wish Marsha were half as smart.
- Her daughter is great in gymnastics. Too bad Beth is on the clumsy side.
- Wouldn't it be nice if Lynn could be a cheerleader like the other girls.
- How did his son get to be such a good soccer player? Jim could learn from him.

Parental attitudes do affect the development of your personality. If your parents outwardly project feelings of disappointment in what you do, it is bound to have an effect on your confidence and self-esteem. If you feel that you are being unfairly compared, or that their expectations of your achievements are too high, try telling them exactly how you feel. It may come as a complete surprise to them.

The Other Side

What if your parents are *consciously* aware of how they feel about you and they *tell* you in statements such as:

- You'll never be what we expected.
- You're a disappointment to the family.
- You've always been a problem to us.

Such comments can destroy your motivation. You can completely lose trust and confidence in your parents. They are communicating the idea that you are not valued. If all your attempts at communicating with them are blocked and you see no possible way to break through, it is time to try a different approach. Concentrating on pleasing *yourself* and becoming a person in your own right.

- Concentrate on what makes *you* happy.
- Trust your *own* decisions.
- Do good things for *yourself.*
- Realize your strong points.
- Set your *own* goals.
- Dare to dream.

ASKING FOR HELP

Many young adults who are caught in an emotional web of a relationship that is falling apart choose to seek outside help by speaking to a teacher, a doctor, or perhaps a school counselor. But how do you know if you need to seek outside guidance in handling your problem? You might want to talk to someone outside the family if:

- You are caught in a hurtful nonproductive pattern of behavior that creates problems and depression.
- You are depressed for an extended period of time.
- You question your feelings regarding your adoption and your place in the family.
- You find yourself turning toward drugs or withdrawing from friends.
- You feel angry, frightened, or desperate about feelings that you can't seem to change.

School counselors are trained in helping you cope with personal and family problems. Often they can see through a suspected problem and get to the target area of conflict. Do not hesitate to make an appointment if you feel the need to talk with someone outside the family.

RUNNING AWAY

Perhaps, as a final solution to your problems, you have toyed with the idea of running away from it all. Whether it is a journey to find your birth mother, or an escape from an intolerable home situation, you feel that running away will be the answer to your problem.

It is true that most young people who run away are fleeing from some sort of fractured family life. They are crying out for help and have nowhere to turn. When no escape seems available and every route is blocked, running away appears to be the only answer for some.

In his book *Running Away,** Arnold Madison lists seven of the most common causes for running away. Do you identify with any of them?

1. Minor family disputes.
2. Trouble at school.
3. Parents whose child-rearing approach is rigid to the point of oppression.
4. Parents who are so permissive that they seem indifferent, uncaring, cold.
5. The runaway is pregnant.
6. Parents are divorced or on the verge of divorce.
7. Youngster has emotional problems.

You could probably add your own reasons to the list and make up another list of feelings about your adoption. What would yours include? Feelings of not belonging? Problems with your adoptive parents? Overwhelming desire to find your birth mother?

There are many reasons why you might be thinking of

Running Away, by Arnold Madison. E.P. Dutton, 1979.

running away. But stop for a moment. Ask yourself these important questions.

- How would I survive?
- Where would I run to?
- Who would be there to help me?
- What kind of life would I live?
- Would I be hurting those I left behind?
- Would I be hurting myself?

Most often, instead of a place filled with freedom and respect (the things you ran away to achieve), you find loneliness and despair. Picture yourself at your new destination. You need a job, money to survive, and a place to stay.

Imagine yourself sleeping on a mat in a room shared by five other people. Soon you will run out of cash. What next? Were the conflicts that you fled from really so terrible? How could they have been worked out? Those conflicts in all likelihood seem small in comparison to what you face on your own in a strange city.

Try to form a realistic picture in your mind about how you would live after you reached your destination. Think about how those you left behind would feel. Following is a portion of a letter that was written to columnist Ann Landers by a mother whose daughter ran away.

"...can anyone imagine how much a mother suffers when her daughter runs away? It is a nightmare. Why did she leave? I cannot understand it. Where is she tonight? Is she warm? Is she hungry? Is she lonely? There is nothing I can do but wait...I have tried so hard to be a good mother but it appears that I have failed..." (From Ann Landers column, October 10, 1986.)

CONSTRUCTIVE COPING

If you were to devise steps to try to settle your conflict *before* you planned your escape route in running away, what would they be? Following are some guidelines to help you:

- Identify your problem.
- Talk about some possible solutions to the conflict.
- Express your hidden feelings about your adoption.
- Explore ways to compromise.
- Make time for each other.
- Choose your communication time wisely.
- Seek the advice of a professional if you need it.

By trying to aquire new communication skills in resolving conflict, you may find that you are creating an environment of respect and trust between you. This is possible when all the parties to a conflict end up feeling good about themselves.

Try to realize that usually the fact of your adoption has no bearing on arguments involving privacy, restrictions, house rules, and the like. Such conflicts are common in most families.

As you know, you will not be living under your parents' roof forever. One day you will be out on your own. Even if things are tough in the present, a sense of the future's possibilities can be a comfort. And although it may seem hard to believe now, these very people that you are in conflict with could turn out to be your closest friends and emotional support system later in life. So try to keep those communication lines open, and new conflicts that might have made your daily living troublesome won't even have a chance to get off the ground. It's worth a try. Don't you agree?

CHAPTER ◇ 5

Searching for Origins

Picture this. You have an overwhelming desire to
contact your birth mother. It is your eighteenth
birthday, and the nagging questions you have had
about your past have surfaced once more. But this time you
plan to do something about it. You tell your adoptive
mother your plans, and she gives you her blessing. The
next step is to obtain your records, so you go down to the
courthouse to get them. The clerk is friendly. She hands
you your true birth certificate and a complete confidential
file of your adoption records. Your birth mother's name
and address are in your file. Contact is made, and a week
later you are on her doorstep. She welcomes you with open
arms, and you wonder...How could you have waited so
long?

What is wrong with this scene? Almost everything. For
one thing, there should be a director in the background
yelling, "Cut!" There should be a floor of cameras and
production people moving about. Because this is not a real-
life scene. It is a movie portrayal.

In real life you would be met with obstacles from the

start. They might begin the first time you tell your adoptive mother your plan. You will have difficulty obtaining your court records because they are sealed and filed away according to law. Sometimes even the best attorneys cannot get adoption records released from the system. The process could take years. And lots of money.

Suppose you do finally find out the name of your birth mother. What now? Do you make the call? Write the letter? What if you are met with cold silence on the other end? This could be rejection for you in the highest form. Remember, your birth mother did what she did for a reason. Would she want to hear from you after all these years?

Those are just some of the obstacles that adoptees face when they make the decision to search for their past. It is important to note that a large majority of young adult adoptees have no desire to look into their biological past. They would never consider starting the legal process to trace their roots. Although they may question certain things about themselves from time to time, they go to their adoptive parents for whatever answers they can get. Unanswered questions remain unanswered. It is no great tragedy to be in the dark about certain facts. To them, their adoptive parents are their "real" parents. Where they live is their only "real" home.

I wouldn't want to try to find out about my past. It's not important to me. So someone gave me up. The ones that took me in are the ones who count. Unless it was for some medical reason, like I've heard happens sometimes, I have no plans to try and find out what is in my records.

Whereas many adoptees have no desire to search, others have but one ambition in life—to find their biological roots.

They want to know many things, such as what their birth mother looks like, what their real religion is, where they were born. Some are satisfied with just looking at their adoption records. They may want to see the reason they were put up for adoption. Even if their adoptive parents tell them the reason, they want to see it written in black and white.

Those who are intent on getting information are referred to as *searchers*. Searchers may just want general information or they may want specific identifying data. Some may want to go the full route and have personal contact with their birth parent. Most experts agree, however, that the adoptee should be an adult before starting a search. The exception would be if there were a medical problem and the adoptee's life were in danger.

David, a thirteen-year-old adoptee, was hospitalized because of a severe kidney ailment. His health was deteriorating fast, and his doctors needed a specific medical background on him. He was a candidate for a kidney transplant, but his birth mother had to be contacted for medical information before surgery could be performed. A court order was filed for the release of David's records. His birth mother was found, and contact was made. David's doctors received the information that was needed to save his life.

GENERAL INFORMATION

Adoptees who are looking for general information are usually interested in their place of birth. They may question the reasons for their birth mother's decision to give them up for adoption. This information is contained in the adoption record, which is sealed and retained by the court.

An adoptee cannot walk in and ask to see his personal adoption record. This can be done only by obtaining a court order, which is a difficult task.

The records are sealed for many reasons. The most important one is the protection of rights of those involved in the adoption: the birth parents, the adoptive parents, and the adopted child.

In her book *Beating the Adoption Game*, Cynthia Martin defines some adoption terms. Following are three terms that might be helpful to you.

Sealed Birth Record.   The birth certificate is amended at the time you are legally adopted. The old birth certificate with the name of your birth mother is then sealed and may not be opened unless specific requirements of the state are met.

Adoption Records.   The records kept by the adoption agency about individual adoptions. They contain names of birth parents and medical information and background on birth parents, adoptive parents, and adoptee. The laws giving you access to your original birth certificate vary from state to state. Few of the laws are specific; therefore most are subject to the individual judge's interpretation.

Good Cause.   Records are opened only for good cause, such as the need for genetic information, or to help you if not knowing certain things is causing you deep psychological problems. Curiosity is not considered sufficient cause.

Perhaps you are thinking that when you get older you would like to begin a search for your roots. You have a nagging desire to know details of your past, but you are afraid to admit this to your adoptive parents. What are some of your worries? Can you identify with any of those listed?

- If I admit that I want to look for my birth parents, my adoptive parents will feel terrible. And then I would feel guilty.
- The emotional pressure of rediscovering my birth mother would be too much for me.
- I would find my birth mother and she would reject me.
- My adoptive mother would never trust me again.
- I might find some terrible secret about my past hidden in my records.
- I might find that I like my birth mother more than my adoptive mother.
- I might "expose" my birth mother by trying to make contact with her.

I always used to threaten my adoptive mother that I was going to run away and find my "real" mother. She would end up crying. I knew that I could get to her that way. Now that I'm older, I really don't want to find my birth mother. Funny thing is...now she would let me go look. But I don't even want to find out.

Sari, 17

ADOPTIVE PARENTS

Let's look at the other side for a moment, the side of the adoptive parents. One of the biggest fears of adoptive parents is that one day their child will want to seek out his/her birth mother. A common feeling of insecurity runs through them—what to do when faced with the question of "searching."

The majority of parents interviewed regarding this admitted that they would agree to the request if the child's desire was so great that it was affecting his/her sense of happiness and well-being. Many agreed that they would help their child in the search. They felt that sometimes just curiosity about the unknown is strong enough to keep the child pushing.

> My girls are only two and five years old, but I am a nervous wreck thinking that one day they might ask to find their birth mother. If my husband and and I have one common worry, it is what the girls will want to do when they come of age.
>
> Judy, 39

> I am a single parent. My children are twelve and thirteen. We were in bitter conflict over the fact that the kids wanted to meet their "real" mother. They knew that I had been in contact with her throughout the years. We fought over this constantly. Finally, I agreed. I made the arrangements to meet her at a park outside of the city. The reunion was awkward at first, but as the day wore on, everyone became more relaxed. The kids answered her questions and they asked her questions about her life. We finally said our goodbyes. My kids have not mentioned her since that day. They were just curious, I guess. We are at peace among ourselves. I feel that I did the right thing.
>
> Gertie, 41

> I say that I will accept my daughter's request to find her birth mother, but in my heart I know that I am

afraid. What if she finds a long lost "bond" with her real mother and never comes back to me? I know that I have to let her try. I might lose her if I don't let her go. The best thing for me is to wait, and hope for the best.

Maria, 40

I have told Mike that if he wishes to trace his biological parents, I would not object at all, hoping that it might help him to feel less isolated or upset about being given up by his natural mother. He has told me, without my asking, that he feels his problems with alcohol may be genetic. Mike has had many sessions of treatment, none of which have worked. The longest period of time he was dry was when he was going to school about six months ago. He was in school for almost eight months and was able to do the work, but for some reason he fell back into the same drinking pattern. It's a very difficult thing to watch.

Barbara, 50

As you can see, adoptive parents are concerned about the idea of letting their children begin searching for their roots. Many parents who appear outwardly tough are actually nervous and somewhat sad about the subject. They are questioning what kind of reception you might receive on the other end. They worry about losing you.

Here you are, their pride and joy. You have had many happy years together as a family. They have raised you the best they knew how, with understanding and unconditional love. And now perhaps she will fall in love with you too. The baby that she gave up over a decade ago is not the same child that she is seeing today. Adoptive parents worry. And they often think along the lines... WHAT IF?

- WHAT IF she likes my son so much that she invites him to stay on with her?
- WHAT IF our daughter sees financial success in her birth mother? WHAT IF she is offered things that we cannot afford to buy her? How will we look in her eyes?
- WHAT IF he thinks his birth father is a better person because he has higher status in the community?
- Our child is an only child. WHAT IF she visits her birth mother who has lots of children? Will she prefer her family over ours?
- WHAT IF her birth mother rejects her? It would be a depressing blow. Could she handle it?

Can you see a parallel of thoughts between adoptees and adoptive parents? Many times, if you communicate your fears to each other, guards can be let down. Knowing how the other person feels can ease the way, when and if the time comes to search.

Felíz Barsky is a psychotherapist and family counselor who practices in Tarzana, California. Miss Barsky specializes in working with adopted adolescents and their families. Besides counseling young adoptees, Miss Barsky is herself one. She speaks not only from a professional view, but from personal experience as well. She says,

"Teens are often concerned that bringing up certain questions about their origins with their adoptive parents would threaten or embarrass them. It is only recently that parents have had support groups available to them where they can express their own unresolved feelings of insecurity and confusion as adoptive parents. They can talk openly about their fears of 'losing' their child to the birth parents.

"However, the adopted teenager's quest for understanding of his origins is merely that; it is a healthy and significant transition in an adoptee's growth and should be regarded by everyone involved as that. The adoptive parents must believe in their child, and in that trust, balance their emotional feelings in regard to their child's interest in his origins and serve as a support system for the child to explore and discover his entire identity."

POSITIVE vs. NEGATIVE INFLUENCES

Studies have shown that if the subject of "search" is treated in a positive way and questions regarding it are answered honestly, the adoptee can be more at peace with himself.

What are some positive or negative ways that you feel might influence a search? Study the list below. Can you think of some other situations that are not included?

Positive	Negative
The adoptive parents agree to help their child in the search.	The search becomes an obsession with the adoptee, disrupting his/her daily living.
The adoptive parents will respect the wishes of the birth parent, if that wish is to be left alone.	The adoptee makes repeated attempts at contact with the birth parent, even though the birth parent objects.
The adoptive parents will follow correct legal procedures regarding obtaining their child's records.	If the birth parent is found to be more successful, the adoptee makes comparisons, and may look down on his/her adoptive parents.
The adoptee will not lie or go behind the adoptive parents' back regarding the search for the birth parent.	The adoptee blames the attorney or the agency worker for the failure to locate the birth parent.

BIRTH PARENTS

Often the common areas of discussion regarding a search are centered on the feelings of the adoptive parents and the adopted child. Little mention is made of the feelings of the birth parent once contact has been made. Imagine for a moment how a birth mother must feel receiving a call fifteen years after having given up her child. Perhaps a letter arrives one day from a stranger, explaining that the baby she gave up years ago is now looking for her. Would she agree to a meeting? Fifteen years! What could have happened to her in all those years? Chances are she has a family of her own. She is living a totally new life. Maybe the fact that she once had a child is a secret buried in her past. Would she want to expose it now? After all this time? It could bring heartache and suffering to her if her "secret" were discovered.

I was contacted on a Friday morning by a woman who said she believed I was the birth mother of her eighteen-year-old son, Donald. My heart started to pound as she described the child. She told me the date and the place of his adoption. I knew she was right. She asked if I wanted to meet him. I told her that I would have to think about it, it was too much of a shock. I had a family with four kids now, nobody knew about "him." But I knew that if I didn't see him I would never again have a peaceful night's sleep. So I called her back and we arranged it. I drove to a nearby town and we met. It was very hard for me. He was tall and had red hair like mine. He seemed happy.... We had a short meeting and then I left. She did a good job with him. I can sleep at night, now that I know.

Marsela, 48

Every adoption story is different. Some birth parents welcome the contact with excitement and open arms. Some refuse it altogether. Letters are returned, calls unanswered.

One of the strongest arguments against the search is the shock a birth mother may suffer from confrontation with a long-buried past. She may have kept the secret from her husband. What would she say? How could she possibly explain it? And most of all, what would it do to her present relationship?

The following question and answer appeared in a column by Dr. Joyce Brothers in *Good Housekeeping*, November, 1986.

Q: I was adopted thirty years ago and recently found my biological mother. Sometimes when I see her she is friendly, other times she is very cold and even wonders if I really am her daughter. What makes her behave this way?

A: Your biological mother may still be suffering from a great deal of guilt and may still feel very conflicted about you. By that I mean that while she loves you and welcomes a relationship with you, you may at the same time be a painful reminder to her of what she still views as a mistake in her past. In the best mother/grown daughter relationships there is love, respect, and closeness, but not a smothering closeness. In most cases this relationship develops slowly, over many years. Your relationship with your mother came upon you both suddenly. You haven't had time to get to know each other, and thus you are both more vulnerable to misunderstandings and hurts.

Try to talk with your mother about her changes of mood and their effect on you. She may not even be aware of her behavior, but if she is, she may welcome the opportunity to discuss it.

Also, examine your own expectations of her. Frequently, adopted children have very idealized views of their biological parents. Then if they search and find them, they can be deeply disillusioned. The more realistic your expectations of a relationship with your mother are, the less likely you will be disappointed.

Be Prepared

Although some birth parents themselves actually engage in a search, a majority of them do not want to be found. For whatever reason, they do not want the past brought out in the open. In such cases, the birth parent's wishes should be respected. You should prepare yourself for this rejection. The reasons why she gave you up could be many. Maybe she was too poor at the time. Or maybe she couldn't handle the responsibility of having a child. You cannot judge her actions, only abide by her wishes. Adoption searches and reunions are emotional for all concerned.

WHAT HELP IS AVAILABLE?

Support groups exist in many cities that provide reliable information about adoption. Support groups offer families an opportunity to see themselves as they really are, and to change if they so desire. Adolescents learn that parents have their faults. Parents learn that their kids are wrestling with a multitude of problems at this stage in their lives.

Specific problems and events that have led to difficulties are discussed. Lines of communication are opened, and trust is rebuilt between family members. The adoptive families receive constructive feedback and attempt to make their adoption situation work. They voice their deep feelings and needs, and they hear from others in the group.

In 1983 the State of New York changed its laws as a result of pressure from adult adoptees. It now has an Adoption Registry in which biological parents and adoptees over the age of twenty can obtain information about each other if the adoptive parents agree. The registry provides the adoptee with nonidentifying information such as religious backround and medical history.

PROFESSIONAL VIEW OF SEARCHING

As a counselor and an adoptee, Miss Barsky says, "I feel that the adolescent adoptee is a child now struggling to discover his/her own identity, which is very difficult because of the lack of integration between past and present. The child is overloaded with feelings of guilt, as well as intense fears of separation, yet has a strong desire to be independent like his peers.

"When a child grows up with half-truths, it is hard to justify the argument that the world is an honest place.

"Adoptive parents should approach their children with openness and honesty and help them to strengthen their feelings about who they really are.

"It is not the relationship with the adoptive parents that usually motivates the adoptee to search for his roots. It is the need to be free to be oneself and to have the power to choose for oneself. Adoptees are not necessarily looking for mothers or fathers. They are looking for 'missing pieces.' They are looking for feelings that seem impossible to describe to other people. We all want to know everything about ourselves. And if we ask, we deserve the right to know."

DECISIONS

When you are older, perhaps you will feel a need to trace your biological past. Try to think about the reasons that you might want to take that journey. Are you curious? What would you gain by satisfying your curiosity?

Let's say your parents agree to help you search for your birth mother. When and if you find her, will you accept the fact that she may not want to see you? Or perhaps even admit that you are her child?

It is important not to be consumed with the feeling that only "biological bonds" are important, that bloodlines are the only lines that count. How many natural parents do you hear of who are unfit to raise their children? Think about it.

Throughout this chapter we have seen different views on the subject of adoption searches and reunions. There is no right answer to the question of whether or not you should trace your roots when you reach adulthood. Every situation is different.

Think about your feelings and the feelings of your adoptive family. Weigh all the possibilities. Try to recognize your motivation, and prepare yourself for the outcome, whatever it may be. Remember, you are the lead in a real-life cast of characters. But there will be no director in the backround yelling "Cut" to stop the scene once it has begun. The decision you make could very well be the most important one you will ever have to make.

CHAPTER ◇ 6

Parents' Views

Meet Andrea. Tall, pretty, dressed smartly in the latest style. She enters the room gracefully and smiles. She sits down across from me and appears ready for our prearranged interview. Her hands tremble slightly, the only sign of nervousness. "You aren't going to use my real name, are you?" she asks hesitantly. I assure her that all contributors may remain anonymous. We agree that adoptive children and their parents would tend to speak more freely about their feelings if their identities remained unknown. I ask if she's ready to answer a few questions about her experiences as an adoptive mother. She says that she is ready, and we begin.

Q: How old are you, Andrea?

A: Thirty-eight.

Q: And how many children do you have?

A: Two daughters, twins...they're in their early teens.

Q: They are adopted?

A: Yes, we adopted them quite early. It was through a private adoption; an attorney arranged it.

Q: Did you know their mother?

A: Yes. My husband and I met her once. She knew that we were going to get the babies.

Q: Did she know that she was going to have twins?

A: Yes. She was only sixteen at the time. Living at home and going to school. It all went pretty smoothly. Everything was worked out before. We were lucky to get the girls so quickly. It was just under two weeks.

Q: You were lucky...?

A: Because we didn't have to wait like a lot of people do. I think the earlier a child comes into a home, the parent/child bond has a better chance to develop. You kind of get a head start on it.

Q: How has the bond developed between you, now that the girls are older?

A: It's grown stronger over the years. I really feel like they're my own.

Q: And your husband?

A: I think he forgets sometimes that they're adopted. He hardly ever mentions it anymore. I don't remember the last time he said anything about it.

Q: Do you forget?

A: No, I think about it all the time. Especially on

their birthday. I alway wonder if their "other mother" is remembering the day.

Q: Do you ever talk about it with the girls?

A: Never.

Q: Why?

A: Well, for one thing...they never bring the subject up with me. They used to when they were younger, but they haven't said anything in a long time. I don't want to be the one to start talking about it.

Q: Why is that?

A: Because I'm afraid, I guess. I know I shouldn't say this, but I don't want them to think of any other mother but me. I think if we start talking about her...you know...kids that age are curious about everything. Who knows what might happen?

Q: So it sounds like you're afraid that they might want to know more about their birth mother if you bring her up in conversation.

A: That's right. I pray that they don't.

Q: You're afraid of losing them?

A: You could say that.

Q: What if one day they come to you and tell you that they want to find out more about their past. What would you say?

A: I know I wouldn't forbid them to look into their past...they'd probably do it anyway. My girls are pretty headstrong. When they put their minds to something together, watch out.

Q: Would you help them?

A: No. I don't think I would.

Q: Would your husband?

A: I'm not sure. He might.

Q: Is there any last thing you'd like to comment on, speaking as an adoptive parent?

A: Well...let's see. Adoptive mothers worry. They worry a lot. The ones who say they don't aren't telling the truth, if you ask me. The way the laws are changing, I guess it won't be too long before the adopted kids will be able to find out anything they want. It will be hardest on mothers like me; we'll be the ones having the problems with it. I love my girls so much that I don't want anything or anyone to get between us. Others might feel different about it, but this is the way I feel.

DOING IT RIGHT

When Andrea and I first met, her main concern was that somehow she'd have to give the names of her kids or the place of their adoption. She was so protective of their identities that I knew what her worry was before we began the interview. She was afraid of losing her children. She admitted that as a parent she has always been overprotective. She said that she and her husband often overdid things as parents because of the underlying fact that the girls were adopted. Although the fact was hardly talked about, they were both overpermissive with the girls and overindulged them with material things. When the girls became sick, even just with a cold, Andrea and her husband became alarmed and rushed them to the pediatrician.

Andrea's feelings are common among adoptive parents. They have a tendency to overindulge their children, especially in the earlier years. Following are some of the reasons parents say they overcompensate:

- They try to prove that they are "good parents."
- They have a fear of one day losing the child.
- They look at the situation as temporary, even though it is not.
- They feel that others are judging them in how they bring up their child.

Adoptive parents give many other reasons why they overdo in raising their children, but generally it appears that they have a long-awaited love for a much-wanted child and a desire to "do it right."

I had no idea what to expect when I first adopted Sara. Now I regard her as my own child. But I know someday I'll have to face that she *was* someone else's child once.

LOOKING IN

Many adoptive parents feel that when a man and a woman have a biological child, the public does not watch as closely how the child is being brought up. They feel that they are often judged by outsiders, or even by family members, on how they rate as parents, something that "natural" parents do not have to face.

• • •

Jake is the adoptive father of Michael, who is seventeen. He has felt over the years that others were always talking about how effectively he was raising his son. He realized that his feelings were somewhat paranoid, but he couldn't help himself. As a result Jake overcompensated in his role as Dad. He bought Michael an overabundance of toys when he was a young child. He overlooked many situations in which his son should have been disciplined.

Jake's insecurity dated back to the time when the adoption agency worker made visits to his home when Michael was a baby. He was always a nervous wreck wondering what she was thinking. Was the baby being taken care of properly? Were the parents' responsible? Did she make the right decision in giving them Michael? Because of this insecurity, Jake aways tried harder to prove to himself and everyone else that he was a good parent.

Most fathers (biological and adoptive) have common concerns. They often feel guilty about not spending enough time with their child. They worry about the cost of the child's education. But adoptive fathers have added concerns. They question: "Does s/he love me like my own child?" "Am I raising him the way a natural father would?" "Will he ever want to look for his 'real' dad?" Adoptive fathers think about the birth fathers, too.

When Bill started playing hockey, I immediately thought of his natural dad. I know who he is. I know that he was a first-class hockey player in school. He would be proud if he knew that his son was taking after him. I want to look him up, to share things about Bill with him, but I don't have the guts to make that call yet. I keep thinking maybe the two would hit it

off. I think I'm cheating them both out of something.
I know I'll put them together one day. I feel I owe it to
Bill.

A STRESSFUL JOB

Parenting is a big responsibility. The job is especially difficult when there is conflict over adoption-related problems. Adults think that if they do a super job as parents
their children will be forever appreciative and turn out
"super." This is often not the case. There could be years of
unresolved conflicts and underlying bad feelings that have
never been openly discussed. These feelings, held inside,
could pop up later in life.

A common problem is for a child to find out by accident
that s/he is adopted. This may occur when the adoptee is
older, perhaps even into adulthood. Perhaps a relative lets
it slip, or it comes up when a medical history is being
traced.

Try to imagine, after years of having no inkling that you
were adopted, that you suddenly learn that the parents
who raised you are not your "real" or "natural" parents.
The shock could be unbearable. How would you react to
something like that? Perhaps it has happened to you. Many
children who learn later in life of their adoption hold a
grudge against their adoptive parents for keeping the information from them. Why, you may wonder, would adoptive
parents keep adoption a secret? Following are some
answers from the parents themselves.

- Too many years have passed without the child's
  knowing. It would be too much of a shock to disclose
  it now.
- The child resembles the adoptive family so much

that it was easy to pretend and not say anything about the adoption.

• Adoptive parents want to be considered the "only" parents the child will ever know.

• They are afraid of losing the child's love if they admit that they withheld the information.

TV MODELS

There is no such thing as the perfect parent except perhaps those parents of the 1950's from the famous TV shows "Leave It to Beaver" and "Father Knows Best." Ward and June Cleaver and Jim and Margaret Anderson were as close to perfect as you're going to get. But in those families the kids were perfect too. Father's word was law. Ward Cleaver's kids answered him with "Yes, sir" and "No, sir." Dinner was at six, and well-scrubbed faces assembled at his table each night. Talk was of the day's problems, like Beaver's lost wallet or brother Wally's new love interest. If life were only that simple...

Don't you wonder how Mr. Cleaver would have reacted to a *real* family problem, such as Beaver's running off to join a religious cult, or Wally's turning to drugs because his mother just informed him that he was adopted? Not too many people might have tuned in, though, because they really didn't want to see what they themselves were experiencing. They wanted to see fantasy, how life was supposed to be in the perfect household.

It's true that the fathers of yesterday and today are not clones of Ward Cleaver or Jim Anderson. They are concerned parents, trying to cope with keeping their families together financially and emotionally. It's a tough job, and an even tougher job for adoptive dads.

My son always screams at me when he's angry, "You're not my father, I don't have to listen to you." It hurts a lot.

When my kid does something extraordinary I'm proud, but I can't help but wonder if it came from his "natural" dad.

FULL CIRCLE

It is difficult for a young child to visualize a parent's weakness. When you were younger, what your parents thought of as right was right in your eyes. If a mother tells her two-year-old that brown cows give chocolate milk, the child believes her. Why doubt it? Moms and Dads are knowledgeable and strong and indestructible. You depend on them for everything. But then, as you grow older, things start to change. You begin to challenge their ideals and to notice little insecurities about them—things you never noticed before. Perhaps your mother is anxious before meeting someone; you know, because you see that she is nervous and jittery before the doorbell rings. And you just learned that your dad had been passed over for a promotion. Your dad? You thought he got everything he went after. Your parents become more like—people—in your eyes.

As you grow older, you may even find that you begin talking and acting the same way they did. They, in turn, start to become more dependent on you. You may find yourself helping them out in little ways, such as doing some shopping for them, or helping to pay the rent on their home or apartment. The shift of dependency bends. Soon you may notice that you are acting more like the parent, and your parents are depending on you like children. And so goes the cycle.

In biological families, the cycle of dependency is often taken for granted. Parents grow older, and it is a comfort for them to know that the children will be there as a support when they are needed. In adopted families, however, there is always that outside concern of the parents that they may one day lose their child to the birth parent.

The hopes and expectations of "forever after" are not always felt by adoptive parents. They do not usually take their children for granted. They express a deep gratitude that their lives have been enriched and made happier by their child's presence. Of course, conflicts and serious problems develop throughout the relationship, but in general adoptive parents agree that they are especially thankful for the chance to raise their kids.

LETTING GO

Some adoptive parents say that they have problems accepting the approaching independence of their adolescent. They see it as having to let go, as being without their child, perhaps stirring up some of the old feelings they had before the adoption.

Miriam knew that she was being unfair in not letting Janet go on the overnight trip with the church choir. She realized that she had been saying no to a lot of Janet's requests lately. It wasn't Janet's fault. At sixteen, she was a smart, sensible girl. She had never given Miriam anything to worry about in the past. But Janet was an adopted child, and Miriam had waited many years to get her. Their years together as mother and daughter had been more loving and satisfying than Miriam had ever expected. And now it was time for Janet to break away, to be with other girls her age.

Miriam was afraid of being left alone, with many of the same feelings of loneliness that she had experienced before Janet was adopted.

Miriam was reacting instinctively. She was trying to keep her daughter close to her in the only way that she knew.

HOW THEY FEEL

In previous chapters, we saw incidents that stir up feelings of anger and concern in young adoptees. Now let's look at how the adoptive parent feels. It is interesting that of the many adoptive parents surveyed, the majority reported many of the same feelings about their hopes and their worries for the future with their adoptive children. Perhaps you feel that your own parents could have additional comments to add to the list below.

What Makes Adoptive Parents—Angry

- Unwanted advice from other family members about their job as adoptive parents.
- Birth parents who try to make contact with the adoptee despite the adoptive parent's objection.
- Prejudice from the public about adoption.
- Racial slurs and remarks about a transracially adopted child.
- Obstacles in the court system when attempting to search for medical or other reasons.
- Children who continually say, "I don't have to listen to you, you're not my *real* parents!"

Concerned

- The thought of possibly losing the child to the birth parent.
- Continuing unresolved conflict within the family.
- Always being compared to the birth parent.
- Jealousy between the adopted child and the biological children.
- Not enough support groups in smaller cities and towns.

Hopeful

- New laws being developed giving adoptees access to more information about their past, if needed.
- A better understanding of adoption by the public.
- More interracial adoptions taking place, giving more children a better chance for a home.

Happy

- When their adopted children are happy and content within the family.
- Successful reunions.
- Being told by their children that they are considered real parents.
- Being able to help others who are having problems with adoption.
- Knowing they have done the best possible job in raising their child.

Gretchen is the mother of Alex, 14, and Christine, 11. She is a single parent. At first Gretchen was a foster mother to the children; after a series of court battles, she won full custody, and recently, guardianship.

Q: Gretchen, your story is most interesting in that you had to go through a number of court battles to be able to keep your children, from the time they first came to live with you. Can you explain some of the circumstances?

A: Sure. My kids are full-blooded Indians. They are half Navaho and half Paiute. They are brother and sister and were born on a reservation in New Mexico. Soon after they were born, they were given up by their parents and taken to a group of Mennonite people. The babies were taken care of well, and it was there that I first saw them.

Q: Did you know that you wanted them when you first saw them?

A: Yes. Nobody else wanted them. The women there were kind, but they were trying to find homes for the children. I fell in love with them right away. I had always wanted kids, but I wasn't married. So I applied as a single parent to be a foster mother.

Q: How did you feel when you first brought the children home to live with you?

A: I wanted to be with them all the time. I used to read to them in this big rocking chair. They couldn't speak English, but they loved it when I read to them. I enjoyed them so much that I didn't like it when it became night and they had to go to sleep. I missed them during that time. I felt the absence.

Q: What happened a few years later when they started to go to grade school?

A: We had some terrifying incidents. One in particular was when their relatives kidnapped them and took them back to the reservation. They hid them, and it was months before I found them. I had to go through the courts to get them back because the relatives wanted them to stay. The judge ruled in my favor. When I got them back, they were malnourished and in bad shape. They had not been taken care of. I fought hard to keep them and won custody. Then I won guardianship, which is even better.

Q: Now that they are entering adolescence, do they ever show a desire to contact any of their relatives or go looking into their past?

A: Yes. In fact we had a reunion recently with their birth mother. We spent time together traveling in a motor home. We all went to Disneyland. Then they wanted to find their father. So I helped them look for him. We couldn't find him because he had remarried and moved away. But while we were searching, we found the kids' half brother. It was nice. They spent time together.

Q: Do you have any concerns or worries for their future?

A: Well, I'm always worried about that law. The one that says when children turn twelve it is their choice whom they want to live with. I worried about it when Alex turned twelve, because he always used to threaten to run away back to his people when he got mad. Now, though, he is very loyal. I know he will stay. But Christine will be twelve next year and I feel insecure about her approaching birthday. The kids have calmed down quite a bit since they know that they have a choice and that I would help them in whatever they wanted to do. We have a special closeness and a friendship that has developed. I'm hoping that it will be enough to hold us together.

The following is taken from a letter written by an adoptive grandmother:

I really have to stop and remind myself that they are adopted, they're so much part of our family.

I recall, the first Christmas Jeffrey was with us, thinking how much his biological grandparents were missing and how fortunate we were to have him to love and enjoy.

When he was about four years old, we were looking at family photo albums and I was showing him pictures of grandparents and great grandparents on both sides of the family. He said, "Grandma, didn't Mom and Dad ever tell you that I'm adopted? So I guess these aren't my relatives." I thought for a while and then said, "Jeff, we adopted you and now it's your turn to adopt the family. If you think you'd like them, I'm sure all these relations would like to be adopted. He turned pages, looked at them and said, "They look pretty okay, Grandma, I adopt them."

Another incident I recall was when Jeffrey wanted to know his *real* name. His dad said, "Thompson." To which Jeff replied, "No, I mean my *real* name. My

friend Kent is adopted, and his *real* name is Gilman."
Jeff's dad said that he really didn't know, but when Jeff
was sixteen they could go to court and have papers
released so that Jeff could find out.

We have had so much pleasure from all our
grandchildren, and each one is very special in his own
unique way. My husband and I feel that adoption is
wonderful, and we're so very grateful that these young
men are a part of our family.

As you can see, adoptive parents worry too. They
wonder how they look in your eyes. They are concerned
about the future and where they fit in.

Even after reading this chapter so far, it may be difficult
for you to see the other side, to understand your parents'
concerns. Perhaps your emotions are running strongly
because of conflict within the family. You may be angry
with your parents and wish that things were different in
your life. You may fantasize about how things would be if
you were living with your birth parents. But try for a
moment to understand *why* your adoptive parents are
concerned, *why* they are part of your conflict.

Biological families fight. The parents worry plenty about
their kids. They worry about curfew, money, the kids'
clothes, their attitudes—the usual worries that occur in
adolescent years. Now take those worries and add to them
the adoptive parents' worries. Of possible threats to run
away. Of continual conflicts within the family over adoption problems. A heavy load for any parent, wouldn't you
agree?

Try to imagine that one day you learn that your parents
have another child living in an undisclosed location. What
thoughts would run across your mind? Will they try to find
him? Is he smarter than I am? Is he better looking or more

talented than I am? If they found him one day, would they still love me? Where would I stand in their eyes?

Alan is a 33-year-old attorney with a successful practice in a large metropolitan city. Alan is also the adoptive father of Janie, who is 4. Alan is white and of the Jewish religion. Janie is black. I asked him to share some of his thoughts and feelings on his role as an adoptive father.

Q: Alan, I know that Janie is only four, but I wonder if you ever think of how things may be in the future, when she reaches her teens.

A: Yes. I wonder what kind of problems we'll come across.

Q: Concerning. . .

A: Well, the usual problems of that age. . .plus the fact that she's adopted. . .also, that she's a different race than I am.

Q: Do you know who Janie's birth father is?

A: Yes.

Q: Does he have any contact with her?

A: No. He tried to a few times, but he didn't get very far. I wouldn't let him.

Q: Why?

A: For one thing—financially. He wants no part of her that way. He walked away from her when she was a baby and wouldn't contribute a penny to see that she'd be taken care of. He lost her that way for sure. The only time he's tried to come around was because he was curious. He wanted to see what she looked like.

Q: So you will not allow him to see her?

A: Not unless he wants to help out. Which he doesn't. I believe he gave up his right when he left her. A once-a-year meeting to see how cute she is or how tall she's grown is not reason enough for me.

Q: What about when Janie is older—say seventeen or eighteen—and says she wants to find her "other" dad. Do you ever think about that?

A: Sure I do. And I know she'll probably do it eventually. If it's really bothering her, I'll try and help her. I'm also prepared for the other thing— you know, color. "You're white—you're not my dad." It'll be coming up sooner than eighteen.

Q: How do you plan to deal with that?

A: I hope by that time she'll consider me her real dad. We're really close now. I love her like my own. I hope the feeling will always be like that. I know it will be on my part.

Q: Do you ever come across a situation, when you are out together, where people make remarks about the interracial relationship?

A: I've never had anyone say anything directly to me about race or color. I have had people make comments about how beautiful she is, how sweet she is. They come up and pinch her cheek and make small talk.

Q: I was wondering how you feel personally about adoption searches once kids come of age.

A: It all depends on the circumstances. I can only speak for myself. I would never *not allow* her to search for her birth father, especially if it was hurting her not to know. But I wouldn't open all the doors for her and push her into it if she wasn't 100 percent behind it. I can't say how she'll be at fourteen or twenty-eight. Who knows what will happen then?

Q: And if she did eventually find him?

A: By then, I hope it's just *her* curiosity. I don't see how they could have any bond between them, other than biological.

Q: So, if they do meet one day in the future, you hope it's just that—a meeting.

A: I hope. But you can't say. You know, people change. It's the future. No one can tell what's going to happen in the future.

A LOOK INTO THE PAST

A number of movies have been made recently with a similar theme: traveling back in time and looking into an era of the past. Some of the films show children going back in time to the years when their parents were in high school. Did you ever wonder what your mother looked like or acted like when she was your age? Chances are, she'd be with her friends, laughing and gossiping about boys and dances. She would have her ideals, her views about what the future held. Maybe she had visions of herself as a mother with lots of children, a business career, a life full of happy, festive times. If she had hopes of starting a family, as many women do, she would not have known then that she was in for some disappointing times. The inability to conceive was indeed written in her future, but she was unaware of it then.

If you could flash ahead some years, you would probably see her differently. She would be waiting for a child, but instead of waiting the usual nine months, her wait was to last for years, two, possibly three or four. But she had no choice. The decision was not hers to make. And then, after a long and hopeful wait, *you* come into her life. Because she had to wait so long, she may now have a tendency to hang on a little harder, to watch over you a little more. It may be true that your lives are clouded with anger and arguments, but beneath the conflict lies basic strong feelings of love and belonging.

What adoptive parents hope for in general is that, putting conflicts aside, their kids will grow into happy adults. They think of their children as *real* children. They hope that they will be considered *real* parents.

As one parent says, "Few successes in life come easily and without effort. When your adopted child looks back on his life and one day says 'Thank you,' you feel a great achievement, a deep sense of pride."

CHAPTER 7

How the Adoption System Works

O ne of the members of an Adoption Support Group was a sixteen-year-old girl who felt that she had been kept in the dark about the circumstances surrounding her adoption. She said, "There is no point in asking my parents questions about my past. They just tell me what they *want* me to know. It's like a planned story, something somebody told them to tell me. They don't treat me as if I have a right to know about myself, so I don't even ask anymore."

Many other young people agreed that not only did they know little of their past, but they knew less about what adoption really is. They were in the dark about how the system works and what their parents had to go through to get them. Some adoptees were familiar with terms that they had heard but did not really know the meaning of the words, such as "special needs child" or "independent adoption."

How often have you heard phrases such as agency worker or black market babies? In this chapter, we shall discuss the different types of adoption that are available and find out where adopted children come from before they are placed in their adoptive families.

We shall also look into some of the steps that couples have to take to be eligible to become adoptive parents. Your own parents did not merely make a phone call one day and get placed on a child waiting list. They had to go through long periods of questioning. They had to open up their home and their lives to show that they were fit and decent people, able to give a child a loving home life.

Agency adoptions begin with the appearance of an expectant mother, who is referred to later as the birth mother. She may be in need of financial or medical help. Often, she is alone and has no place to stay. The expectant mother is introduced to a social worker who is assigned to help her through her pregnancy. The social worker will advise her on her options and what decisions she will have to make regarding the baby. The mother may be frightened by her situation and have no family support. She may look to the social worker for emotional support and for answers to her questions, such as:

- What does it take to provide for a child? Will I be able to do it if I'm on my own?
- Would the child have a better chance with another family?
- How will the decision affect me? Will I regret it if I decide to give the child up?
- If I decide to keep the child, how will I be able to finish school, or work to support us?
- What are my rights now and later if I decide to give the child up for adoption?

The past few years have seen a rise in the number of unwed mothers choosing to keep their children. Usually they have some parental support, either in the form of financial assistance or child care. This allows the mother to finish school or work in a job while raising her child.

A vast number of expectant mothers, however, have no one to turn to for emotional or financial support. These women decide to sign a "relinquishment of rights" to the child, and the biological father consents to give the child up. It is then that the agency moves to put the baby up for adoption. A number of agencies are available, including the Department of Public Welfare, the Bureau of Family and Children Services, and the Division of Social Services.

AGENCY ADOPTIONS

For prospective adoptive parents it can be a very long wait. Even after a couple is put on a waiting list for a child, it can be years before they are called in for a meeting with a social worker. And first they must go through many steps just to get into the system and be eligible for consideration. Prospective parents may have to answer preliminary questions over the phone when they first make the call, such as:

- How old are you?
- Do you have any other children?
- How long have you been married?
- How is your health?
- What is your religion?

Some couples never make it past the first phone call. They are intimidated by the questions and feel that they are too personal in nature. If they knew the type of questioning that would come later when they were seriously being evaluated, they might not consider the preliminary questions so personal.

Those who are serious, however, are more than willing to answer the questions. They receive an application and are asked to join a group meeting. This meeting is designed to acquaint couples with the adoption process and the kinds of children who are available for adoption.

Prospective parents have a number of meetings with a social worker over a period of about six months, during which time the social worker determines the couple's reasons for wanting to adopt, their personalities and parenting ability. They go through a home study, a series of interviews between the applicants and the social worker. Following are some of the questions they may have to answer.

- Why do you want to adopt?
- How do you feel about children?
- How were you brought up as a child?
- What is your life-style?
- What type of work do you do?
- What is your yearly income?
- What are some of your past experiences with children?
- Do you have a strong marriage?
- What do you expect of a child?

The home itself is examined carefully to be sure that it is safe and clean and could accommodate a child. The social worker assesses the couple: Do they show enthusiasm? Are they stable people? Will they be tolerant? Will they be flexible? The interviewer may notice certain questionable attitudes that arise in conversation, negative characteristics such as prejudice, immaturity, or indecisiveness.

If the interviewer decides that the couple or the home would not benefit the child, the couple are rejected. They are given an explanation and are free to apply elsewhere.

If the interviewer finds that the couple can offer a loving home for a child, the procedure begins and a child is looked for to place with the family.

Placement

Most applicants want perfect, healthy babies, but there is a great need for adoption of "special needs" children. Most children so labeled have some characteristic that presents too great a challenge for an average adopter. The child may be of school age or of a minority heritage, or have a physical or learning disability.

If a child is found for the couple, they are given information about the child and a meeting is arranged. A main concern of the agency is that the parents feel comfortable with the child. After the child is placed in the home, the social worker makes periodical visits and observes the child's development.

Finalization

The social worker sends a referral to the court to finalize the adoption after the child has been in the home at least six months. A few months later, the parents appear in court to sign and finalize the adoption. Agencies have postadoption services that are available to adoptive parents after the finalization for any help that may be needed in the adjustment process.

INDEPENDENT ADOPTIONS

Independent adoptions are usually handled through a third party, such as a lawyer or a doctor, who acts as intermediary between the biological mother and the adoptive parents. Names are usually kept confidential.

The third party screens the expectant mother and questions her, but not as deeply as in the home study interview. She is asked about her family background, her medical history, her feelings about the child, and her reasons for giving the child up. Legal paperwork must be completed on both sides.

In some cases the adoptive parents agree to help pay the mother's expenses, such as food, clothing, and medical bills, during the pregnancy. Agencies do not provide full payment for medical expenses. They can only suggest welfare as a means of support for the expectant mother.

Jill and her husband, Derek, decided to make a private adoption. They advertised through a newspaper in a distant town. When their ad was answered by an expectant mother, they retained an attorney to handle the arrangements. Jill and her husband had to agree to a number of stipulations. They had to agree to pay all medical expenses and lodging and clothing allowances during the last three months of the mother's pregnancy. In turn, the expectant mother would place the baby with Jill and Derek and sign away her rights to the child. Jill says:

It was not easy. I felt that at any moment she might change her mind. I was walking on eggs, afraid to say or do the wrong thing. I even drove her to her doctor appointments and sat in the waiting room. It was awkward. We didn't say much to each other. She always seemed to be looking me over, wondering if she was doing the right thing. Even after the baby was born and we brought her home, I was still afraid that the mother would show up at the door to take Charlene back. The baby is eighteen months old now, but I still don't believe she's truly ours.

OPEN ADOPTION

When prospective parents and birth parents make arrangements with no attempt to hide identities, it is called open adoption. In some cases, birth mothers want to select parents for their child. They may want to place the baby directly with adopters or work openly with a third party. The parties may share letters and pictures about the child and speak openly with each other. Many believe that open adoption is in the best interests of the child.

BLACK MARKET BABIES

Black market babies are babies who are bought and sold outside the law. No attempt is made to provide safety for either the parent or the child. Secret arrangements are made, money is exchanged, and the whereabouts of the child becomes unknown. No documents are filed with the courts to enable these children to be traced. Sometimes they are sold in foreign countries. Obtaining a baby or child through the black market is risky; however it still goes on in the U.S. and abroad.

INTERNATIONAL ADOPTION

International adoption refers to children who are born abroad and placed in the U.S. for adoption. There are many abandoned or orphaned babies and children around the world. You only have to turn on the TV or pick up a magazine to see ads about them. Many couples decide that they would like to give one of these children a home.

Before such an adoption can be approved by a court of law, certain consents must be obtained. The child is asked to consent to the adoption if he is legally old enough to do so (at least twelve years old). The consent of the birth parents (both mother and father) is needed. If this is not available, the guardian or next of kin is acceptable. These consents must be obtained properly, usually through an attorney. Many requirements of the state and federal governments and the foreign country must be met.

Some states have adoption agencies with direct ties to child-placing services in foreign countries.

As we have seen, there are various ways for a child to be adopted. The main concern of those involved is guarding the well-being of the child and placing it in a receptive, loving home. As one agency worker says,

It is not as easy as people may think. There are many requirements that prospective parents must meet even to be considered as adopters. Some couples may think that they will pass easily, that they are "right" for the job. But the agency people may feel different-ly. They may reject the couple for any number of rea-sons. We try to find the best possible combination between parent and child and bring them together. It may be a long and frustrating wait, but the end result is worth it when you see the look on the parents' faces. There is a lot of love there. There's no way to describe it. You just know you made the right decision. And so did they.

CHAPTER 8

Adoptees Speak Out

The following are transcribed excerpts from a therapy session conducted by Felíz Barsky, M.A., M.F.C.C. The young people were all adopted teenagers, between the ages of fourteen and seventeen.

MARSHA

Ever since I was six, seven years old I began to tell stories about who I was, who my parents were. I told everyone a different story. I was always lying about anything to do with my past, family history and stuff. I just kept making it up along the way; it was very hard because I had to remember what I told whom. I just couldn't seem to tell the truth about myself because I felt as if I never had any history, no roots, no past, like an alien. I would always hang out with friends who had close families so that I could feel like part of a real family. No matter who I was with, I'd never feel I really belonged anywhere. I wanted a family so badly... I became obsessed with it, so much so that when I was fifteen I left home and moved in with my boyfriend (who was from Mexico) and his parents. They had a typical Latin home, very warm and loving, with the smell of tortillas and soup around the house. It felt wonderful. They were very poor but very close, and I tried to blend in and be a part of their lives. But it never *really* worked, I wasn't related. I wasn't related to anyone. My parents felt like strangers to me, even though I loved them very much. My brothers and sister were very nice, but I just didn't feel really connected to them and I wondered if I would ever feel connected to anyone.

MARCINA

Whenever I would hint that I was curious about my natural parents, my birth parents, my adoptive mom would become hysterical. As a matter of fact, everyone in my family would act weird. They kept saying, "Why do you want to find your birth parents? You've got the best parents in the world; look at all they did for you. They were always there when you needed them. Besides, if your mom and dad had wanted you they would have kept you. You should be thankful for such good parents. You're lucky they put up with you after all the hell you've put them through." I always felt that if I was too bad they would send me back somewhere... I don't know where. So sometimes I tried to be as bad as I could just to get it over with and have them reject me. I would go from being very very good to very very bad. I just wanted my parents to approve of me, so I was always doing things for attention. My dad (adoptive father) liked art, so I would do a lot of art stuff and try to get him to notice my pictures, but it never felt like I was really getting paid attention to. Then I would try to find boy-friends who would pay a lot of attention to me. It felt like I was always hungry, like...this feeling like I needed something very badly. Since I've been in the teen group I see that other people have felt like that, but before then I really never talked to anyone about being adopted, other kids, I mean. I was like a secret.

JOHN

My adoptive parents are very overprotective, especially with my adopted sisters. They are too much...they are too involved...it's like they're trying to make up for some-thing. And I had a strong feeling that talking about my birth parents would *not* be a good idea; I could see my mom tighten up and get cold and my dad just sort of shrugs and says I'm lucky I went to a good family. He always tells me I better be careful not to get a girl pregnant so she won't have to give up our baby for adoption. That makes me wonder if my real mom was very young, maybe my age. I would never give my own kid up...that's for sure.

KURT

I left home the first time when I was fifteen....I was always taking care of myself, even when I lived at home. I was kind of a loner. I really never thought much about being adopted until recently, although I always felt kind of different, kind of strange, weird, as if I just don't fit in anywhere or with anyone. I did always wonder if I even looked like anyone in my real family. I wondered if my real father liked motorcycles, because my adoptive father hated them and I was really into them. I wondered also if my real mom would have liked me a little better than my adoptive

mom did. . .She was kind of cold of me. I think she was
kind of upset that she couldn't have her own kid and in her
family background the only people who are really accepted
are the ones related by blood. So I think she was more into
obligations like, you know, making everyone on the
outside think she was just the best mother. But it was all
just a show. . .she just didn't like me. I guess I remind her
of something, like not being able to have a baby. I think
she just adopted me to save her marriage, because my dad
really wanted kids. But we don't talk much in our family. I
really never talked to anyone until I came to a teen group.
It feels a little better now to be able to hear what everyone else is going through.

PATTI

When I was younger, I thought, "Why did my mom give
me up? Was I bad, ugly, horrible, why didn't she keep
me?" I would have all kinds of fantasies about why, like she
was too poor to keep me or too sick, and that it really broke
her heart. I wondered if she had been pretty. . .if I looked
like her. Lots of times I was curious about having my own
baby, what I would do. I think I've taken a lot of chances as
far as not using birth control goes because I kind of want a
baby so I can keep her and not give her away. I don't really
talk to anyone about my adoption. My parents used to say
that I was "special," that I was "chosen," that they picked
me out of a lot of kids who needed homes. I could have just
been left in that orphanage and no one would have taken
me. I guess I'm lucky. My adoptive parents always gave me
everything I wanted, the best schools, lots of clothes, a
nice car. . .everything I ever wanted. And they pretty
much let me do whatever I wanted. But sometimes I wish
we didn't have so much. Like some of my friends, when

I go over to their house it feels better, more homey, more family-like. Their moms are kind of strict with them, they've got curfews and stuff and they have a lot more rules than I do, and they don't get all the nice things I do, but there's just some kind of feeling, I don't know, just something that feels more like a family. Sometimes I wish I was in their family and that we had...I don't know. It's hard to describe. Being adopted *is* different. I never really talked to anyone about it before except once when I was around nine or ten. I told my best friend about it, and she said to me, "If your parents get really mad at you, can they still take you back to where you came from? Gosh, *that* would really scare me...you better not do anything to make them mad." I thought about that for a long time.

CHAPTER 9

Making It Through

Let's begin this final chapter with part of an imaginary dialogue about a confrontation between an adoptive mother and her daughter.

MOTHER: I'm sorry, but you can't spend the weekend with Cynthia and her family.

DAUGHTER: You never let me go anywhere. You treat me like a small child.

MOTHER: No, you are wrong in thinking that.

DAUGHTER: No, *you* are wrong, Mother. I'm seventeen. I should be able to go places with my friends. I've never given you reason to distrust me.

MOTHER: But what if something happens?

DAUGHTER: What could happen? Why are you always trying to hang on to me?

MOTHER: Why are you always wanting to run someplace?

> DAUGHTER: Because I can't stand the way you try to overprotect me. I feel smothered. When I turn eighteen—I'm leaving anyway!

Do you remember reading in Chapter 6 about adoptive parents' feelings? What do you think this parent was thinking when she refused to let her daughter go on the weekend trip?

If you recognize the mother's fear of letting go, you are right. Perhaps some of her pre-adoption fears of loneliness and being without a child are showing through. How could you have altered this conversation, using some of what you have learned in previous chapters?

> MOTHER: I'm sorry, but you can't spend the weekend with Cynthia and her family.

> DAUGHTER: Why?

> MOTHER: What if something happens?

> DAUGHTER: Mother, if you think that I'm asking to go places rather than be here with you, you're wrong. I'm seventeen. I feel that I should have the freedom to be with my friends. I love you. *Our* relationship as mother and daughter has nothing to do with the relationship I have with my friends. I hope that you will trust me and give me a chance.

Knowing how other adoptive parents feel about their relationships with their children may make it easier for you to recognize similar problems that occur in your own family.

You may also be able to change a potential conflict over upsetting comments by using some of what we talked about in Chapter 2.

MARK: I was hoping you guys would include me in the plans for the Halloween party.

CHRIS: To be honest, the reason we didn't ask you is that we felt it might be too much for you. There's a lot of running around to get ready, and we didn't think there was anything... well, you know...we thought we were doing the right thing in not asking you.

MARK: I would have liked to help you out. I may be in a wheelchair, but I'm sure there are things I could have done, like help out with the refreshments or help plan the music.

CHRIS: We didn't realize that you wanted to help. But now we know for the next event that comes along.

MARK: Thanks. There are a number of things I *can* do, and I really do want to be included.

As you can see, it is possible to change the way a person thinks or feels about you by using newly developed attitudes.

HOW TO COPE

Coping with adoption-related problems takes time and understanding, but they can eventually be resolved. To begin resolving them, you may have to be willing to make some changes in your life. Stop for a moment. Take a personal inventory of your own situation. Ask yourself these questions:

- Can some of my current disagreements be worked out? My severed relationships mended?
- Can I start to move toward fewer strains and tensions in my personal life?
- Would I be willing to reaffirm friendships and strengthen ties of trust and affection?
- Can I learn to think of my adoptive parents as my real parents in the sense that they are the ones responsible for raising me from childhood into adulthood?
- Can I accept the fact that I am not responsible for the circumstances surrounding my birth? That I had no control over my being given up for adoption?

By attempting to change some of your thinking, you have taken the first step in achieving peace with yourself and your feelings about your adoption. How you feel about yourself makes a difference in the way others respond to you. If you attempt to open up clogged lines of communication, you improve your chances for an honest and trusting relationship with your adoptive family.

Adoptive parents who have positive relationships with their children project those feelings. The adoptees then grow up feeling good about themselves and those around them. Many adoptees eventually go on to become adoptive parents, opening up their homes and their lives to a waiting child. New dimensions are added to their lives, and so on down the line of generations to come.

Think about your own family. Ask yourself: What are we

really to each other? Are we strangers? Or are we in-
dividuals living and working together for a happy and
peaceful coexistence?

The purpose of this book is to show that problems concerning adoption are widespread. You are not alone with
your feelings and concerns. From the birth mother to the
social worker to the adoptive parent to YOU the adoptee, a
circle of lives have been affected by this process called
adoption.

The time will soon come when you will be free to leave
your family and walk away on your own. You will be free to
search for your roots, free to make your own choices.
Coping with your adoption may seem like a problem to you
now, a major problem. But as you grow older and are out in
the world on your own, you will be dealing with other
major problems as well. We all hope for lives of perfect
health and serenity, but it is unfortunate but true that we
will meet with problems of unemployment, sickness, and
even death of friends and loved ones. These are also part of
life's experiences. What may seem like major problems to
you now—family arguments or insults about your adoption—may seem just minor inconveniences in retrospect.

Throughout this book, much of what was discussed was
the difficulties and worries of adoption. But the truth is
that the adoption process is something to be admired. The
most wonderful part of adoption is that someone, after
much thought and consideration, made a choice, and that
choice was to present a child to a family and a family to a
child. The date or the time of the beginning of the relationship is not as important as the fact that a new family
unit was created.

Many adoptees wait years and then one day look back on
their childhood with mixed feelings. They wish that they
had seen or done things differently. They look back and

begin to appreciate much of what was done for them. But do you know what? *You* don't have to wait years. There are no laws or codes that adoptees have to be adults to look back into their lives. You might even want to do it now. You might want to look into your own family and discover ...Maybe I have overlooked the good. Maybe I can re-connect the feeling. Maybe it hasn't been so bad after all.

Bibliography

Anderson, David C. *Children of Special Value*. New York: St. Martin's Press, 1971.

Bank, Stephen P., and Kahn, Michael D. *The Sibling Bond*. New York: Basic Books, 1982.

Berman, Eleanor. *The Cooperating Family*. Englewood Cliffs, NJ: Prentice-Hall, 1977.

Berman, Claire. *We Take This Child: A Candid Look at Modern Adoption*. New York: Doubleday, 1974.

Burgess, Linda Cannon. *The Art of Adoption*. Washington: Acropolis Books, 1976.

Buscaglia, Leo. *The Disabled and Their Parents*. New York: Holt, Reinhart & Winston, 1983.

Capaldi, Frederick, and McRae, Barbara. *Stepfamilies*. New York: Vision Books, 1979.

Caprio, Dr. Frank S. and Frank B. *Parents and Teenagers*. Secaucus, NJ: Citadel Press, 1968.

Friedenberg, Edgar Z. *The Vanishing Adolescent*. Boston: New American Library, Beacon Press, 1969.

Galinsky, Ellen. *Between Generations: The Six Stages of Parenthood*. New York: Times Books, 1981.

Gardner, Dr. James E. *The Turbulent Teens*. Los Angeles: Sorrento Press.

Gilbert, Sara. *Trouble at Home*. New York: Lothrop, Lee & Shepard Books, 1981.

Gilman, Lois. *The Adoption Resource Book*. New York: Harper & Row, 1984.

Ginott, Dr. Haim G. *Between Parent and Teenager*. New York: Macmillan, 1969.

Hartog, Jan de. *The Children*. New York: Atheneum, 1969.

Hendin, Herbert. *The Age of Sensation*. New York: W.W. Norton & Co., 1975.

Kibanoff, Susan and Elton. *Let's Talk About Adoption*. Boston: Little, Brown, 1973.

Kohl, Herbert. Growing with Your Children. Boston: Little, Brown, 1978.

Krementz, Jill. *How It Feels to Be Adopted*. New York: Alfred Knopf, 1983.

Maddox, Brenda. *The Half-Parent*. New York: M. Evans & Co. Inc., 1975.

Madison, Arnold. *Runaway Teens: An American Tragedy*. New York: E.P. Dutton, 1979.

Martin, Cynthia. *Beating the Adoption Game*. San Diego: Oak Tree Publishers, 1980.

McCoy, Kathleen. *Coping with Teenage Depression*. New York: New American Library, 1982.

McNamara, Joan. *The Adoption Adviser*. New York: Hawthorne Books, 1975.

Pogrebin, Letty Cottin. *Family Politics*. New York: Mc-Graw-Hill, 1983.

Powell, Douglas H. *Teenagers: When to Worry and What to Do*. New York: Doubleday, 1986.

Powledge, Fred. *The New Adoption Maze and How to Get Through It*. St. Louis: C.V. Mosby Co., 1985.

Raymond, Louise. *Adoption and After*. New York: Harper & Row, 1974.

Sarason, Irwin G. *Guide for Foster Parents*. New York: Human Science Press, 1976.

Schimel, John L., M.D. *The Parent's Handbook on Adolescence*. Highlands, NJ: New World, 1969.

Schowalter, John E., M.D., and Anyan, Walter, M.D. *The Family Handbook of Adolescence*. New York: Alfred Knopf, 1979.

Schultz, Susan Polis. "Love, Live and Share." Boulder, CO: Blue Mountain Press, 1980.

Winder, Alvin. *Adolescence: Contemporary Studies*. New York: American Book Co., 1968.

Woolfolk, William and Joanna. *The Great American Birth Rite*. New York: Dial Press, 1975.

Zagone, Frank. *How to Adopt Your Stepchild in California*. Berkeley: Nolo Press, 1985.

Index